Out of the Real
Tham & Videgård Arkitekter

Edited and with an essay by Johan Linton
Photographs by Åke E:son Lindman

Birkhäuser
Basel

Table of Contents

Founding Principles

The history of architecture in Sweden is characterized by an oscillation between foreign influence and national tradition. It has often been said that international architectural tendencies are modulated there by economic constraint and a cultural affinity for nature. One Swedish architecture firm in the early 21st century whose work embraces both local and international contexts is Tham & Videgård Arkitekter.[1] Fluid thinking and an affinity for the contemporary have led them to a distinctive way of interpreting Swedish traditions.[2] In a short time and despite limited budgets they have created a body of work that has attracted attention both nationally and internationally, to an extent few active Swedish firms can match.[3] Their most well-known projects include their office interiors for Snowcrash, the *Karlsson House*, the *Archipelago House*, the *Tree Hotel* in Harads, and *Kalmar Museum of Art*, which won Sweden's foremost architecture award, the Kasper Salin Prize.[4] They have also been gaining recognition for an increasing number of projects, exhibitions, and lectures in other countries.

See pages 168–169,
26–41, 146–159, and 56–75.

In the most important survey of 20th century Swedish architecture to date, *Att bygga ett land* (Building a Country), the chapter title for the most recent period, 1975–98, takes the form of a question: The End of the Middle Way?[5] The title indicates a shift in the climate and practice of architecture in Sweden just prior to the founding of Tham & Videgård in 1999. The distinctiveness of the firm's work, the way it relates to both domestic and international architecture, makes a more thorough presentation of that work relevant. It is in this light we might also view Birkhäuser Verlag's initiative to produce this book.

Bolle Tham and Martin Videgård grew up in Stockholm, both of them in families of architects. They were both educated at the Royal Institute of Technology (KTH), but each has had additional training at other institutions of higher learning, both in Sweden and abroad.[6] As students they shared some courses, but had already met before starting architecture school. Before graduating they collaborated on an open architectural competition to design a new public library for the town of Turku, Finland. Though they did not win, theirs was the only Swedish proposal to receive commendation, an experience that encouraged them to continue the collaboration by opening their own office.[7]

At the time, architecture in Sweden was dominated by a number of large and well-established firms, on both the design and construction side, and there was little opportunity to work in the field without the constraints of this establishment. It was common for development and construction firms (some of the largest in the world) to rely on architects only for building permit drawings, or to improve certain aesthetic aspects of a project. The developers' dominance contributed to a steady narrowing of the role of the architect. The tradition of architects guiding a construction project through all phases of design and construction was broken in many ways. At the same time, Sweden's system of construction management at risk had its advantages, including relatively high technical standards and effective production

City Library, Turku, Finland, Open international competition, 1999. Facade 1:100.

methods. And the modern tradition of maintaining basic quality standards through building codes and regulations lived on, a reflection of the idea of the welfare state—a society in which all were guaranteed a decent home.

Bolle Tham and Martin Videgård have said that as they were entering the profession they found few Swedish architecture firms to be attractive in relation to their view of architecture and creative aspiration. Their teachers in architecture school had been critical of the situation, too, but there seemed to be few who could convert their dissatisfaction into concrete action. The founding of their own firm may be seen as a reaction to this state of affairs. In other European countries they had found an architecture of greater earnestness and fewer compromises. They were also influenced by international architectural developments, for example through the discussions among the group of architects who put out the journal *Mama* (1992–2000) and theorists such as Tom Sandqvist and Sven-Olov Wallenstein. In their own practice, the young duo wanted to find a way to reclaim the initiative and responsibility in the construction process that seemed to have been lost by Swedish architects. They also wanted to explore ways of building that would be anchored in a broader context of contemporary architecture.

A founding principle for the new office was to approach architecture's basic issues independent of ideology or convention. Central to their thinking was the conviction that architectural ideas are not really tested until they confront reality, and the corollary notion that reality always provides opportunities for architecture. They were convinced that every serious commission, however limited in scope or budget, could generate architectural qualities. These principles led them to establish the goal that every project would be built. In the areas of responsibility that Swedish architects often relinquished to the developer or builder—budget, technical systems, construction methods—they saw opportunities. For two architects with an otherwise understated manner, it was a bold, uncompromising, and proactive attitude.

Even a cursory study of the firm's work reveals the importance of the ongoing exchange between Bolle Tham and Martin Videgård. While at many larger firms the staff contributes to the preliminary concept development, here the original ideas are essentially generated through the exchange between the two principals. The staff then takes part in developing that initial reading. Whereas in many firms the principals often come to specialize in different roles, Bolle Tham and Martin Videgård are both generalists who are comfortable in all of those roles.[8] In this regard they could be contrasted with, for example, the firm A4, established in the late 1950s, who became leaders in the development of structuralism in Sweden. One of A4's four founders, Ragnar Uppman, advocated the benefits of an organizational structure in which the members develop different relationships to architecture.[9] Tham & Videgård have perhaps more in common with Sven Backström and Leif Reinius, internationally known in the 50s for their so-called star buildings. They claimed to have benefited from frequent confrontations over differences of opinion. But at the same time, they worked very closely together, and they even say they used to switch desks in order to exchange perspectives on their projects.[10] To follow the development of Tham & Videgård as a firm is to follow a conversation between its two principals, one that begins with shared values and develops rather in the confrontation with empirical evidence than conflicting viewpoints. That conversation has also continued outside the office in their teaching and lecturing at architecture schools in Sweden and abroad.

Early Work

Though Tham & Videgård was established around a library project, the firm's first years were characterized by designs for interiors and single-family homes.[11] They received several such commissions as soon as they opened in 1999, and by that fall they had begun work on the first project that would become widely known. Stureplan is a hub of nightlife, business, and communications in Stockholm. Tham & Videgård were asked to renew the plaza's temporary outdoor summer cafe.[12] Their

Restaurant Box at Stureplan, Stockholm 1999–2000.

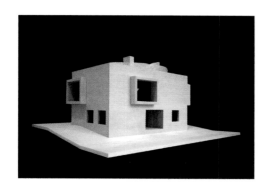

Ugglero House, Kungsängen 1999–2002,
model scale 1:50, entrance level, upper level.

See pages 168–169.

Snowcrash, Office and showroom,
Stockholm 2001.

solution was a mobile kitchen and serving pavilion, a box made of canted planes of perforated aluminum. The form, material, and construction of the box are derived from the functional requirements of the cafe and the character of the site. Its sloped surfaces, for example, shed rainwater and create a form that distinguishes it from the surrounding buildings. The perforated aluminum promotes ventilation, allows the pavilion to glow with light at night, discourages graffiti, and reduces the weight of the structure for easier transport. There is also some visual correlation to the play of light and shadow in the rusticated bases of the neighboring buildings. The pavilion's metallic character, say the architects, is an attempt to resonate with the site's temporary elements—the vehicles that populate the plaza: cars, buses, bikes.[13] In the end it is neither building nor vehicle, but something else entirely.

Another important project from the fall of 1999 was the office's first single-family home, the Ugglero House.[14] Although it took a while before the house was finally built, and although it is not among the firm's well-known and published homes, it was nevertheless an important experience for them, and there are obvious references to it in several later projects. It gave the architects an opportunity to explore the Swedish building tradition, the relationship between building and nature and between content and form, movement through different levels, window types, the use of color, and how to deal with municipal authorities. The Ugglero House was also an early example of the firm's attempt to work through issues of sustainable building.[15]

The second year in the life of the practice, 2000, began with two important projects: the Karlsson House and the office and showroom for Snowcrash. Despite their differences, both projects manifested the firm's working methods, each in different ways, and both garnered attention in professional circles.

In their work on the Ugglero House, Tham & Videgård had expressed the desire to create "a modern barn."[16] With the *Karlsson House*, which was again a low-budget project, they got another opportunity to test that notion. Its form and construction play on the tradition of Swedish barns, and their references for the project included architect Bengt Lindroos's widely known survey of warehouses.[17] At the same time, their treatment of the building type is free and unconventional. Inside, the organization of spaces follows the spacing of the roof trusses, with a series of skylights that give the sequence of rooms a rhythmic variation in ceiling height. On the outside, the entire building—including the roof—is clad in wood siding painted with traditional Falun red distemper. What's more, the windows are fitted with a kind of plank shutters that screen the sun and give the simple building volume a buoyant and charged expression. In spite of its finely wrought architecture, the home's budget was comparable to that of a standard prefab tract home.[18]

When it came to their interiors for Snowcrash (now destroyed), it was the time schedule rather than the budget that was limited. To make matters worse, the client wanted to wait as long as possible before finalizing the program. The architects' solution was both simple and effective. At the center of the light-filled open-plan office they created a core of rooms with assigned functions connected by circulation space painted in dark colors. This core included mechanical rooms, meeting rooms, and rooms for individual work. It was wrapped in a screen of semitransparent, silk-screened, floor-to-ceiling glass panels. The interplay between light and dark, between openness and enclosure, created a spatial tension in the office that was especially tangible to one in motion. At the same time, the flexible glass walls meant the client could wait until the last moment to decide on the final division of rooms. Tham & Videgård's design achieved efficiency and functionality with strikingly simple means. In addition, the solution corresponded well with the client's idea of mobility and progressive, experimental corporate culture.

Expanding Experiences

In the year 2002, Tham & Videgård would take some important steps toward establishing their presence on the architectural scene. The Snowcrash offices opened in

Office of Tham & Videgård Arkitekter, Stockholm 2002.

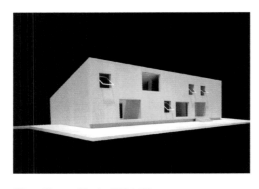

Blom House, Nacka 2001–03, model scale 1:50.

Karlsson House, Västerås 2000–02, concept model scale 1:100.

the fall of 2001, and shortly thereafter the project was honored with the CoreDesign Award, a new international distinction for strategic design.[19] At about the same time, the project was published in Sweden's professional journals of both architecture and interiors. One review called it "the year's most extreme [interior] in terms of space and material." [20] It is also clear from the reviews that the project impressed with aesthetic and sensual qualities beyond the radical expression captured by the photographs. Both the Snowcrash interiors and Karlsson House brought the firm attention in a variety of international contexts as well.[21]

During the same period, Tham & Videgård left their original offices on Åsögatan to create a more suitable space, a couple of blocks away, on Blekingegatan. In a centrally located building from the 1960s, they transformed an introverted warren of office cells into an open, brightly lit space that communicates with the street outside. They are still there today. Although the conditions for their own office were in many ways different from the conditions for the Snowcrash project, some parallels may be drawn. For the Tham & Videgård office, too, they created a generous perimeter space for office work and presentations of current projects, while meeting rooms and service functions were consolidated into an irregular aggregation at the core, where again they used dark colors.

A new kind of commission came to the firm at that time: an addition to an apartment building on Industrigatan in Stockholm. The existing building had not fully exploited the allowed floor area ratio of the property, and Tham & Videgård proposed that it be expanded toward the courtyard, with the addition clad in glass to maximize the daylight in the apartments. One of their references for the project was Pierre Chareau's Maison de Verre. Though it was never built, the design was a first foray with multifamily housing projects, a project type that would become a noticeable segment of the firm's work. The same could be said of work they did in 2002 on an urban planning project for Almada, on the Mar da Palha due south of Lisbon, an invited competition they did together with Bolle's father, the architect Klas Tham, as part of an international team of consultants.[22] Both projects demonstrate Tham & Videgård's determination to apply their ideas on projects of a larger scale.

In the fall of 2003 they began work on two more single-family homes that would come to be among the firm's most significant projects. One is the House K, a long and narrow two-story home in a residential neighborhood outside of Stockholm. The other is the Archipelago House, a single-story vacation home on a pristine island site in the archipelago outside the same city. Despite the projects' differing conditions, there are clear connections between them, and connections to other Tham & Videgård work as well. We could note, for example, the recurring theme of the long and narrow single-family home. In the case of the Karlsson House, the form of the house was at least in part dictated by its simple framing, which made use of the wooden roof trusses commonly found in traditional Swedish barns. The architects worked creatively within this repetitive framework to create spatial variations. In House K we find a similar treatment of the oblong volume, illustrated (as the Karlsson House had been) with a conceptual sketch model.[23] For the Karlsson House they had used a simplified wooden model with a section that showed the light wells created by the different skylights. The model for House K is an abstract white volume in which the various boxes and open spaces that make up the home are interwoven like a three-dimensional puzzle.[24] It perhaps represents a further advancement in the conceptualization of the architects' approach to space.

The Archipelago House, too, could be grouped among the firm's long and narrow single-family homes. Unlike the two-story houses we've already discussed, this one's single story did not provide the same kind of opportunities for compression and expansion of the interior space. In this case the oblong sequence of spaces has been disjointed and shifted along a diagonal displaced forty-five degrees, and the variation of spatial volume—including daylight openings—occurs horizontally rather than vertically. The expansion and compression of space is achieved by shifting or misaligning the rooms and then joining them along a diagonal path. As in their other oblong homes, the architects play with varying the space along the path of circulation, but in the Archipelago House those variations are horizontal rather than vertical. The shifting of the building mass contributes another important quality: the glass wall that opens onto the deck and the view beyond takes on a zigzag form that helps weave together the interior and exterior spaces. Making gradual transitions, or the dissolution of the boundary between inside and out, is a recurring feature of Tham & Videgård's work.

While they were busy with House K and the Archipelago House, an opportunity also presented itself to work on a more compact home. In the spring of 2004, they began studies for a duplex—Double House—in the town of Danderyd, outside Stockholm. As with the other single-family home projects, they were able to make use of prior experiences in developing their ideas. The Double House has elements of both the Ugglero House and two neighboring homes in Hässelby that at the time were waiting to be built. As in the Ugglero House, variations in the ceiling height again create spatial tension, and projecting windows with deep niches amplify the perceived thickness of the walls. And as with the Hässelby houses, the bedrooms of each twin house are arranged along one side and connected by a hall or corridor space.

What distinguishes the Double House from the firm's earlier compact homes is its circulation. Each of the twin homes is built up around a spiral movement that spans four levels. Each level has one primary space. The smaller bedrooms and bathrooms are grouped along the spiraling circulation space. The scheme is designed to heighten the experience of this movement. For example, the ground-level hallway found in the Hässelby houses has been adapted here, narrowing as it approaches the large kitchen in order to emphasize the room's spaciousness and wealth of daylight. The ascent to the second level begins at the far corner of the kitchen, where a stair rises under a light well and lands at the corner opening into the living room, a vantage point that maximizes the perceived size of that level's primary space. The arrangement encourages us to climb the spiraling path and experience the home from its most generous viewpoints. Finally, the path up to the roof terrace is designed as a semifreestanding stair with a sculptural presence in the space that further accentuates the ascent to the top. This kind of careful treatment of the circulation path through general spaces recurs in several of Tham & Videgård's projects. Perhaps the most well-developed and distilled example is their large home for the Ordos 100 project, whose rooms are arranged in a spiral that rises gradually around a central pentagonal stairwell.

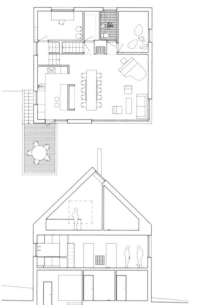

Houses J & S, Hässelby, Stockholm 2003–04, perspective, upper level and section.

The First Big Building

In August of 2004, after five years in business, an opportunity arose that would give Tham & Videgård their first chance to realize a larger building. The architects themselves have pointed out how the competition for *Kalmar Museum of Art* came at just the right time. They had built enough to be able both to develop and to realize ideas for a somewhat larger and more complex building. The competition ended in December, and by early 2005 their proposal had been awarded first place.[25]

See pages 56–75.

One of the jury's reasons for selecting their scheme was its relationship to the site. Tham & Videgård's way of using buildings to shape a site is often governed by their thinking about how to form space. An example is House K, which they describe as a "wall just thick enough to hold a home."[26] The long and narrow building, whose depth is hard to judge from the outside, divides the lot in two, clarifying both the space of front and the space of the rear. With the Kalmar Museum of Art, too, the building is part of a conscious redesign of the site, though the architects' approach is rather the reverse of that for House K: in order to as far as possible *avoid* dividing up the relatively small city park, they chose to limit the building's footprint and build up instead.[27] That decision had other consequences both practical and spatial. There were archeological remains to deal with on the site, and this would have been much more difficult with a sprawling plan. With a taller building it would also be possible to create dramatic views through the park to the castle, the old city, and the waters of the Baltic Sea. The scheme also allowed for a greater consolidation in the

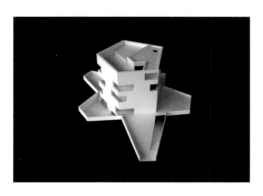

Ordos 100, Inner Mongolia, China 2008–, model study, scale 1:50.

organization of spaces, which would facilitate better logistics and circulation in the building. Like House K, the art museum was conceived as a distinct rectangular volume clad in black plywood panels. Among the few reference images included in the presentation boards they submitted for the competition were photos of House K's facade and the architects' model for the house as illustrations of how they intended to treat the museum's facades. In Kalmar, this facade system was chosen to create effects of light and shadow that relate to the foliage of the park's trees.[28] To maintain the subtlety of those effects achieved in House K, they gave the museum's facade the same black stain.

Tham & Videgård engages with the culture of architecture as a living, evolving heritage, offering inspiration—and to which one is challenged to contribute. One example is the facade system for the Kalmar Museum of Art. Based on Herzog & de Meuron's facades for the Fotostudio Melanie Frei in Weil am Rhein, from 1982, Tham & Videgård have reworked the system, adding horizontal nailers that back the bottom edge of each plywood panel to prevent warping and to achieve new visual effects. They used a version of this system on the Archipelago House as well, thinning it to a semitransparent screen that wraps the deck. The three projects—*House K*, *Kalmar Museum of Art*, and *Archipelago House*—show Tham & Videgård working with a detail taken from contemporary architectural history and developing it further. They explore the many possible variations that system has to offer in much the same way they studied (for the Karlsson House) the practical and visual effectiveness of board-and-batten siding as a roofing material, or of traditional Falun red paint.

See pages 178–179, 56–75, and 26–41.

House K, Stocksund 2004–05.

House K provides a link between the experience of two outdoor spaces: not until we're inside the home is the space behind it revealed. In the same kind of way, the museum offers us an exclusive chance to experience the space of the tree canopy that hovers over the park. In both the house and the museum we are confronted with the second level as soon as we enter the building. House K has two openings between its levels, though the path between them—a U-shaped stair—is largely hidden. In the Kalmar Museum of Art, however, the stair that connects the levels is exposed, the entire stairwell open to the entrance. One of the key ideas for the museum project is this vertical ascent from level to level, the gradual climb into the crowns of the trees and the discovery of new views as we rise. By the time they began on the museum, Tham & Videgård had already worked with the vertical movement between levels several times, including the Double House and the (never executed) renovation of House Z.[29] Another thing the museum has in common with the firm's prior work is its thrift: despite its sophisticated climate control and security systems, the construction cost per square meter was basically no more than for a typical single-family home.[30] As in previous projects, the architects followed the construction process closely, and found that on several occasions the builder attempted to change details because they were unusual, only to discover that the more conventional solutions would have been more expensive.

The jury announced the results of the competition in February 2005, and the building opened in May 2008. There were emotional reactions locally to what some considered a misguided violation of a sensitive cultural environment,[31] and the controversy may have contributed to the delay as well. The clarity and strength of Tham & Videgård's scheme and its solid anchoring in practical construction, however, made it possible to complete the project with the intended qualities intact. The architects have remarked in retrospect how close the final result is to their original proposal. They learned from the experience how charged a public building project can be, and how much media attention can be generated by conflict over such a building. In the end their work with Kalmar Museum of Art demonstrated the extent of Tham & Videgård's ability to deliver on larger projects.

The building, which had been the object of some concern to the local population throughout its planning and construction, received praise upon completion. In 2008 it was awarded the Kasper Salin Prize as the year's best building in Sweden. It was shortlisted for international awards and was featured in foreign architectural journals.[32] All that attention likely had little effect on the firm's design work, but it did expand their network of contacts and lead to new opportunities. Step by step, Tham & Videgård were broadening their international presence, including lectures and exhibitions, and now through commissions outside Sweden as well.

One widely discussed aspect of the museum, both during and after its construction, was the new building's relationship to the Swedish modernist Sven-Ivar Lind's little restaurant, Byttan, that was to be preserved. Tham & Videgård may be said to have chosen both accommodation and contrast. Their basic approach was to see their project as a new construction rather than an addition, and consequently to treat the old restaurant pavilion as a separate design, a significant work of architecture to be treated with respect. The new museum, with its monumental height and dark facade, establishes a clear contrast to the restaurant. At the same time, though, the museum is planned to adjoin the restaurant in a functional and effective manner. And in spite of the design differences, the proportions of the new building seem to harmonize with the old. In the competition jury's statement, they discerned an affinity between the two in that the new building's boxy form seemed to have some kinship with Sven-Ivar Lind's pavilion for the Paris Expo of 1937, which he designed at about the same time as the Byttan.[33] As in some of Tham & Videgård's previous work, there is kinship too with the traditional agrarian buildings of the Swedish countryside. The museum could be seen as a kind of log cabin granary or storage loft for art, where simplicity and frugality are driven to their logical extremes, but with such skill that the sense of being in the presence of *architecture* is never compromised. Traditionally such tall storage buildings were often symbolic of the wealth they contained, and were given an aesthetic treatment accordingly. Tham & Videgård's competition presentation included references to exhibit spaces "stacked on top of one another," to "lofts," "planks," and to a "consolidated volume and simple construction."[34] In later descriptions of the project, the architects would refer to Klas Anshelm's museums and to Charles Saatchi's industrial galleries as sources of inspiration for their informal qualities and well-lit spaces.[35]

Larger Projects, New Responsibilities

In retrospect, it is clear that the Kalmar commission opened the door to a new kind of client and led to successively larger projects. The architects have described how in their work on the museum they studied the park in terms of circulation paths and sightlines, establishing a foundation that would allow them to treat the building as an integral part of a larger context. The next step for the office would be a series of projects that would allow them to work with such aspects of space more elaborately. In 2006 they were commissioned to develop a preliminary sketch for a housing development outside Södertälje. The site was zoned for thirty-five "freestanding single-family homes" surrounding a seventeenth-century estate called Glasberga Manor.[36] The plan also called for the streets in the area to be designed to slow through traffic and create conditions that suited the local residents. The scheme has a clear ecological profile, in keeping with the directives of the zoning plan. The project, though it has yet to be built, has already made an impression on several of the firm's later designs.[37]

Tham & Videgård chose to base their Glasberga scheme on the character of the street, where they saw the greatest potential to achieve a strong result with an economy of means. Whereas the Karlsson House had taken inspiration from a traditional barn, this time they studied the street space of traditional small-town Sweden—it too is an important element in the country's architectural heritage.[38] The architects had given the Karlsson House a uniform volume by cladding the entire building, walls and roof, in board-and-batten siding. At Glasberga they created instead a uniform *space*—a kind of morphological complement to the *Karlsson House*—by enclosing the entire length of the street space with a continuous wooden fence. Instead of single-family homes, they proposed duplexes, oriented every house with its gable end facing the street, and located them so those gables became part of the street fence. By manipulating the height and slope of the fence, they could vary and fine-tune the degree of enclosure all along the street. They also chose to forego

See pages 66–67.

Glasberga Housing, Södertälje 2006.

See pages 168–169.

the usual division of the street space into different zones for travel, parking, curb, and sidewalk; instead they gave the street a single continuous surface that would be accessible to drivers but still support other activities. The attached duplex homes each have three bedrooms and simple floor plans in which we can sense the architects' interest in designing the path of circulation, choreographing our movement. Right from the entrance, for example, there is a stair that ascends into a vertical shaft space lit from above by a skylight.

Another Tham & Videgård project with an urban design aspect is their architecture school for the Royal Institute of Technology (KTH) in Stockholm—a commission they secured by winning an invited competition in 2007. Among the qualities that impressed the jury was their proposed building's relationship to its site.[39] The project is also significant in that the building is much larger than the museum in Kalmar, another step in the firm's development toward projects of increasing scope.[40]

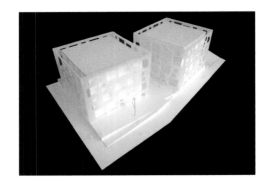

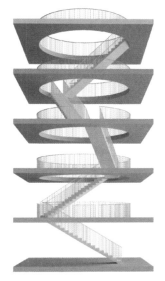

Västra Kajen Housing, Jönköping 2009–, model 1:100 and study of stairwell.

In the spring of 2009, Tham & Videgård were also invited to take part in a competition to design an apartment building on Västra Kajen (the Western Quay) in Jönköping.[41] The competition brief suggested a number of slab buildings on a strip of land along the waterfront, a scheme that would divide the view of Lake Mälaren among as many apartments as possible. Behind these residential buildings was an existing commercial development that included an eight-story administration building. Tham & Videgård were the only competing firm to go beyond the suggested scheme of slab buildings. After a site analysis, they had found the buildings proposed in the competition brief too small in relation to the scale of the surrounding open spaces and existing buildings. Searching for a solution that would be more suited to the site, they developed a scheme with two boldly cubic buildings. By rotating the cubes, they created a more liberal relationship to the neighboring buildings, and established a directional axis toward the water. The proposal garnered first place, and the jury praised the firm's ability to create a rich and distinctive character with simple means. They called the buildings' stairwells "sensational" and highlighted many of the scheme's environmental and energy conservation strategies.[42]

The Västra Kajen buildings—Tham & Videgård's first freestanding apartment buildings—show approaches and strategies evolved from previous projects. The architects took advantage of the big buildings' volumes to work with the vertical circulation inside. The depth of the buildings allowed each to have a central interior courtyard, a kind of social lobby or atrium crisscrossed by flights of stairs that create a complex vertical movement. The atrium of one building is square in plan, the other round. The effort to create opportunities for social encounters among building residents in the courtyards was complemented by the addition of a guest apartment and group activity spaces. The apartments have generalized designs with straightforward, orthogonally ordered layouts, some of which allow residents to walk a loop around their apartment. All of them have balconies with a view of the water. These balconies are staggered from one plan to the next, giving each one a double-height space. Around the outside of the balconies, the buildings are wrapped in an outer semitransparent layer that strengthens the impression of a consolidated volume, while filtering the light that shines into and out from the buildings. The scheme again demonstrates the architects' interest in the relationship between inside and out, in making the boundary with the surrounding space diffuse and indeterminate.[43] Just as the courtyards have been given different forms, so too the facades are colored differently to give each a distinctive, individual identity.

A New Scale

One of the new, larger-scale projects that came to Tham & Videgård at this time was a parallel commission in the town of Södertälje. Shortly after winning the architecture school competition, they were among several firms asked to develop preliminary new housing and urban design schemes for a complicated site in a strategic location.[44] The brief from the city called for sensitivity to the context, but also for urbanity and contemporary architecture.[45]

Södertälje Apartment Tower, 2007.

The project in Södertälje is interesting in many respects. It represents another step forward for the firm. For the rather small and constricted site they proposed three buildings linked together by an elevated plaza area that would deliver the desired urbanity.[46] One of the three is a boldly designed twenty-two-story apartment tower that would be eighty meters high. Until this project, Tham & Videgård could have been categorized by the Swedish tradition of straightforward, reductive design. Their work had been controversial at times, as the reactions to their Kalmar Museum of Art or their interiors for Snowcrash attest, but it had always remained within the boundaries of a kind of Swedish restraint. Their tower in Södertälje is indicative of a shift. Their thinking seems to have turned away from the conventions of moderate scale and understated design. At the same time, it could be argued that their striking scheme is in part rooted in Swedish or Nordic traditions.

The tower illustrates how their thinking around the issues of sustainability had developed in tact with their broadening experiences of architecture and construction. Instead of technical innovations or cutting-edge mechanical systems, the tower design is based on simple observations about the conditions for living well. From a historical perspective, it is only relatively recently that Scandinavians have been able to heat their homes year round. In the past they had to let some parts of the home remain unheated during the winter. Tham & Videgård took inspiration from this fact and tested its applicability in a modern residential tower. They created a fully insulated interior core that extends the full height of the building. An uninsulated terrace floor slab surrounds this core at each level, shifted and rotated to different angles from one floor to the next. These terraces have been finished like a kind of glazed, semi-insulated balcony spaces that prewarm outside air before it enters the apartment interiors. The twisting means that each level has some balcony space on top of the apartment below. The result is a small and well-insulated apartment for the winter half of the year that doubles in size during the summer. The transition from interior to exterior occurs in three stages, from insulated inner core to glazed terrace to open balcony. The middle zone is something contemporary, and yet reminiscent of the glazed verandas of the nineteenth century.

The building's form emerges from a concrete and straightforward treatment of apartment living without much regard to the standard solutions or established conceptions of residential design. While Tham & Videgård may have been inspired by Swedish or Nordic tradition in the apartments themselves, the height of the building suggests a rather different approach to the design task. The Södertälje project is also an example of how the firm works with variations on earlier themes. The tower and the two other building blocks in the scheme are rotated one to the next, as in the design for *Västra Kajen* in Jönköping. We have already noted several projects that make use of terraces and vertical movements, and several that are based on simple, clean geometry. In Södertälje, the reflections and experimentations come from their experience of earlier projects, reworked into schemes that explore the possibilities of contemporary architecture. The tall building with its rotated glass boxes stands like a revelation far removed from the tradition of housing in Sweden. Nevertheless, the firm's working method and fundamental ideas are still in many ways quite close to those that produced the Karlsson House, even if the result has a different relationship to its context.

See pages 194–195.

Vällingby Parkstad, Stockholm 2010.

Tham & Videgård continued on this new track with their proposal for an entrance building for the Vällingby Parkstad housing development. The design was the result of a project to convert a former office park for the Vattenfall electric company outside of Vällingby into a residential neighborhood.[47] To more clearly announce the new character of the area, the developers launched a competition for a tall entrance building that would serve as a landmark for the new community. They also changed the name of the area from Råcksta to Vällingby Parkstad (Park City).[48] Tham & Videgård proposed a residential tower that branches out four levels up into four identical arms.[49] The base of the building holds shops and offices, while the upper branches are for apartments with terraces. At the base, where the context is that of urban space, the building plan is deep to accommodate the needs of commercial users. Higher up, in the four branches, the architects have established a scale more suitable for living. They have described the project as a "new typology." The tower is a contemporary addition that distinguishes itself from the surrounding buildings. They refer to it as a "tree building," a name that both resonates with the idea of the park city and describes its distinctive form.

According to the architects, the form is the result of a contextual and spatial analysis. They wanted to free up green space around the building by reducing its footprint. They also wanted to create apartments with the views afforded by living in a tower and the intimate outdoor rooms that come with row houses. Besides the tree reference, Tham & Videgård have called the space between the building's upper branches "an inverted variation of the unique outdoor space formed beneath the Eiffel Tower in Paris."[50] One way to read that statement would be to consider their building an interpretation of the famous tower turned upside down.[51] It could also be seen as referring to the role the Eiffel Tower has played in building identity for the city of Paris.

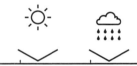

Emergency Architecture, Exhibition at NAMOC, Beijing 2009.

When the office began working on their proposal for Vällingby Parkstad, they had just completed work on another project that dealt with giving structure to a new housing development. In the fall of 2008, they had received an invitation from the National Museum of China in Beijing to take part in an exhibition of emergency structures for natural disaster relief efforts. While the task was in many ways different from the one in Vällingby, through the analysis of the architects both projects came to deal with buildings that would have a kind of gathering effect in a newly constructed mixed-use area. When Tham & Videgård received the invitation, they contacted experts from organizations such as the Swedish Rescue Services Agency and the Swedish International Development Cooperation Agency to gain an understanding of the conditions for building temporary camps in response to natural disasters. As a result of those conversations, they based their proposal on three fundamental lessons learned by experience about the spatial environment of those camps.[52] First was the importance of quickly making competent and strategic long-term decisions about the future development of the catastrophe area. Those decisions are rarely made by architects, which often makes reconstruction and redevelopment efforts, and the subsequent transition into a permanent urban structure, more difficult. The second fundamental lesson is that relief camps often remain in use much longer than intended, sometimes for decades, and become essentially permanent. And third, the camps need to do more than just satisfy physical needs; the refugees' frustration at the lack of visible change and progress as well as poor conditions for social interaction, is also a huge problem. The architectural and urban qualities of the quickly constructed camp can therefore be as significant as its strictly functional attributes.

The architects proposed a simple structure that would strengthen the urban fabric of the relief camp in a variety of ways in both the short and long term by providing a special place reserved for public functions. The design resembles a large pyramidal tent that has been turned upside down. Its height and size were such that it could serve as an orientational landmark for the social and public activities of the camp. It would also serve as a symbol of the ongoing relief effort. It would provide shade in warm climates, protect from inclement weather, and gather rainwater. The structure's fabric is stretched over a frame of four long poles that come together to bear on a central base and are stabilized by steel wires. The fabric could be given different colors to further facilitate orientation within the camp. If the camp evolved to become a permanent settlement, the simple tent structure could be replaced by a more sophisticated building or urban public space.

Once more Tham & Videgård had used an iconic image of a monumental building and turned it upside down. Beyond the comparison with the contemporaneous project in Vällingby, we could also draw parallels with one of the firm's earliest projects, the little restaurant pavilion in Stureplan. It is no stretch to note that both are simple, nonpermanent, tent-like structures designed for a dense urban environment. Though both the structures and their contexts are quite different, there is a kinship in the logic of their design—another illustration of the continuity in Tham & Videgård's thinking about architecture.

Each of the projects we've studied in this section has an urban planning aspect, though none can be strictly categorized as an urban planning project. Tham & Videgård have said they consider urban planning to be a structural and strategic exercise, rather than one of design and specificity. It remains to be seen how they will handle their first urban planning project when it comes. They did make a decision that borders on urban planning when they chose not to participate in a widely publicized competition to design an addition to the Stockholm Public Library: they said the new construction would have a greater strategic benefit to the city if it were located elsewhere.[53]

Living with Nature

Söderöra, Summerhouse, 2005–07, plan.

See pages 56–75.

See page 7.

Despite their success developing their practice toward ever-larger projects, Tham & Videgård have maintained a solid foundation of work with private homes.[54] At essentially the same moment they learned they had won the competition in Kalmar they were starting work on a new commission to design a small vacation home on the island of Söderöra in the archipelago outside Stockholm. The project conditions in terms of materials and accessibility recall those of the Archipelago House. In both cases there was no vehicular access from the mainland to the island site, so construction materials had to be transported to the island by boat and then moved to the site manually. In other regards, the project briefs were different. Whereas the Archipelago House had been about staging an expansive flow of space, in the Söderöra project they worked with compact, concentrated spaces. Nevertheless, both include references to the Swedish veranda—a glazed space between the interior and exterior of the home. A closer look at Söderöra reveals other references that contribute to the complexity of what appears on the surface to be a simple house. For example, despite obvious differences, there are connections to the *Kalmar Museum of Art*. Both buildings are consolidated forms with a definite vertical orientation that is manifested, among other ways, in the use of skylights. Though the character of their facades differs, both are also clad completely in black, which helps neutralize their visual force. An essential feature of both buildings is their use of room-sized openings onto the surrounding natural landscape.

On this last point we can also draw similarities between Söderöra and the way Tham & Videgård worked with the relationship between building and nature in their earliest projects. The upper level of the *Ugglero House* consists of a single open space with large windows that form niches oriented in each of the four cardinal directions. The windows are placed in a rotating fan-blade pattern, another expression of the architects' interest in the dynamics of space. Söderöra is an obvious reworking and refining of the same scheme: the fan-blade motif is applied to a square room and the niches have become independent spatial appendages that alternate from one side of the house's climate barrier to the next.[55]

Another unusual but significant example is their tree house for the Tree Hotel, a small inn in northern Sweden. Here, too, the program is limited: a place for two to spend the night up under the crown of a tree. Tham & Videgård based their interpretation of the task on the high-tech aspect of outdoor life today, with products and materials that make spending time in nature as practical and comfortable as possible. They took inspiration from the somewhat contradictory tension between sophisticated equipment and untamed nature by using a high-tech structure to limit the impact on the sensitive northern forest environment.

Tree Hotel, Harads 2008–10, illustration.

The simple tree house is clad in a surface that is mirrored on the outside and transparent on the inside. From inside we can see out, but the reflective exterior causes the little cabin to disappear among the trees. The scheme also included an ultraviolet film that would prevent birds from flying into the glass. It is interesting to note that the inspiration for the building—a tree house—is the same as that for the tower they designed immediately thereafter for Vällingby Parkstad.[56] In both cases the idea of living up in the trees has resulted in designs with spectacular features but entirely different scales and characters.

*See pages 90–101, 26–41, and
131–145.*

Another private home worth a closer look here is their renovation of a large turn-of-the-century apartment on Humlegården Park in Stockholm. Like the house on *Söderöra*, they began work on the project in 2006, during the same period in which the *Archipelago House* was being finished. The *Humlegården apartment* is unique in several ways, but one of its most distinctive features is the new parquet flooring of ash stained in various bright colors. Tham & Videgård have pointed out that the scheme makes reference to predecessors in Swedish art and design from time periods with a richer decorative idiom than that of pure modernism, including the work of Carl Larsson and Josef Frank. One could also mention the rural vernacular tradition of painting architecture in vivid colors, as in the kurbits style of richly decorated floral motifs used in Dalarna. The architects moreover note how the colors refer to the park outside, and the archive for the project includes photos of leaves in the same brilliant autumn colors found in the flooring.

See pages 116–129, and 180–181.

Thus Humlegården, Söderöra, and the Tree Hotel can all be seen as examples of strategies to give nature a presence in the interior of the home. Two more single-family homes from the same year (2006), the *Garden House* and the *Botanic Garden House*, are notable for the careful treatment of their relationship to nature. In the Garden House, the exterior walls are seen as part of the surrounding garden, so the home within becomes an interstitial space wrapped in vegetation. And the facade of the Botanic Garden House has trellises that can be raised and lowered, dissolving the boundary between inside and out.

Cultural Buildings

It would probably be hard to overestimate the importance for Tham & Videgård of the win in the Kalmar Museum of Art competition. One concrete result was a commission to design a new branch museum for Moderna Museet (the Swedish Museum of Modern Art) in Malmö. The brief called for a new building to adjoin and include an old brick power plant constructed in 1901. In 1988 the plant had been converted to the Rooseum art gallery with funding from a private collector and financier. Tham & Videgård's task was therefore a renovation project with strict demands on climate control and security. The time schedule from the first preliminary design study to the opening of the new building was limited to only eighteen months. Adapting the old building to a somewhat new and different organization was a demanding challenge, and their solution was simply to construct a new building inside of the old one—a strategy that also paved the way for some innovative design work.

Moderna Museet Malmö, 2008–09.

The project for Moderna Museet Malmö was different in many respects from that for the museum in Kalmar, and yet there were similarities. One important experience the architects could transfer directly to the new commission was the significance of a cultural building for creating identity and generating activity in the local community and throughout the region. Aside from issues of technology, security, and project management, the architects made two primary contributions to the new building. The first is an orange-red entrance box that includes a cafe, museum shop, and a new gallery. The second is the reorganization of the interior spaces around two new stairs that creates a loop between the ground-level turbine hall and the upper gallery spaces. These two basically separate measures provide an interesting illustration of Tham & Videgård's working method. The combination of simple, clear, strong forms and dynamic spatial organization is characteristic of their architecture, and because of the particular circumstances of the project, in this instance the two strategies have been implemented in different parts of the building. We have already seen examples of the boxy volume in the firm's work, beginning with their cafe pavilion on Stureplan (2000). Despite differences in form and function, the Moderna Museet addition is another metal box with a perforated surface.[57] In Malmö it is clear that from early on the architects were looking for a strong volume with some kind of depth effect: one of the first schemes had a tall box form with an undulating, folded surface. The same scheme included a low vaulted opening onto the street, a connection that is to some extent preserved in the final design, in which the entrance hall is only separated from the street by a perforated screen.[58]

When it comes to the layout of the building, we can again note the importance of their work with vertical circulation and stairs in particular. In this case, the ascent up the stairs is confined to a high, narrow space whose walls provide a separation between the three galleries of the turbine hall. This constricted passage is a simple way of accentuating the spatial tension in the transition between the lofty turbine hall and the lower-ceilinged, enclosed upper gallery spaces. It's a variation on the spatial principle of the Karlsson House, in which the single oblong space is broken by transverse cuts through the structure.

Stockholm Concert Hall, 2009–, model scale 1:100.

Tham & Videgård's acumen for designing public buildings would manifest itself again in further competition wins. Before work on the museum in Malmö was complete, they were invited to participate in a parallel commission to design a renovation and addition of considerably more sensitive nature. The Stockholm Concert Hall, Ivar Tengbom's monumental neoclassical building on Hötorget, needed to be altered and expanded to meet the organizational and functional demands of a modern performance venue. [59]

The firm's analysis of the program and vision statement embraced the original idea of the existing building and the measures that had already been planned for it. To improve the acoustics, the building's roof needed to be reinforced, and that led the architects to consider the possibility of placing the new program spaces on top of it. That approach worked well with the building's existing circulation system and with Tengbom's original vision for a concert space that would be open to the light of the sky.[60] Tham & Videgård's proposed addition would realize that dream, providing views over Stockholm and up into the sky. Behind their scheme lay an analysis of the site and the Concert Hall's role as an urban monument. Their use of the roof made them the only one of the invited firms to satisfy the building program without taking space from adjoining buildings, thus allowing them to preserve the hall's stature as a freestanding object in the urban environment.[61] Their delicate handling of the cultural-historically significant Concert Hall and its complicated technical requirements makes this ongoing project one of the firm's most complex and sophisticated projects so far.

Bergman Center, Fårö 2010, exhibition space.

See pages 90–101.

Several months before Tham & Videgård learned that their proposal for the Stockholm Concert Hall had been selected for continued study, they were invited to participate in yet another competition for a cultural venue. This time it was a new building for the organization dedicated to managing and developing the legacy of film director Ingmar Bergman, the Bergman Center Foundation, on Fårö, the small island off the north coast of Gotland in the Baltic Sea. As in Stockholm, they were one of four firms invited to compete.[62] The task was to transform the two perpendicular buildings of a former school into a visitor's center with a screening room, exhibition space, cafe, library, and local cultural museum. It was again a renovation project, but this time it was the cultural landscape that needed to be preserved rather than a historically significant building.

Tham & Videgård joined the existing buildings under a single large new roof and were able to accommodate the desired program without changing the layout of rooms in either. They removed several partitions but left all the bearing walls in place. Still the scheme doesn't appear to be subservient to some existing spatial structure. The exterior has the form of a great barn-like volume clad in black roofing felt that is reminiscent of *Söderöra*. Spatially, the architects worked with the tension between the entrance court in front of the building and the park space at the back, facing the sea. These two spaces are divided by the long black building, but linked together by its entrance hall, which is entirely open in either direction. We have seen a passageway playing such a prominent role in other Tham & Videgård projects, including the Ugglero House, Moderna Museet Malmö, and House K. The black exterior is set off by a red interior, its color descended from traditional cinema decor, though the tone in the cafe and reception is somewhat brighter. The exhibition space, on the other hand, is as black as a camera obscura.

We can assume that one reason Tham & Videgård won the competition was their success in incorporating the existing buildings into their scheme. According to the

See pages 56–75, 196–197, and 168–169.

jury, they also succeeded in uniting simplicity and a robust utility with poetic qualities that suggest the work of Ingmar Bergman.[63] Like the *Kalmar Museum of Art*, the *Bergman Center* resonates with the Swedish tradition of building. Besides Söderöra, this calls to mind the *Karlsson House*, which also made modern use of traditional red paint, though this time the color has been deployed on the interior. In their description of their proposal, the architects explicitly state that they wanted to both tie their design to the local building tradition, with steep, gabled roofs, and yet introduce something new and unexpected.[64] As in their work with the Stockholm Concert Hall, they have again housed all of an organization's more or less complex operations within a unified and clearly legible building volume.

Layered Clarity

As already suggested, the field of architecture in Sweden underwent a significant transformation during the last decades of the twentieth century. The state began to lift its strong guiding hand, and the Swedish "culture of unity" became increasingly pluralistic and international. Housing construction began to recede from its central role in society and "the Swedish Middle Way" reached the end of the road, at least in the form for which it had become known.[65] It was during this period of transformation that Tham & Videgård started their practice. They have described how they were fiercely committed to reality—both in subjecting their projects to the limitations of the real world and in their determination to get them built. It is obvious that from the very beginning they had the ability to understand their clients' needs and to respond to those needs with architectural solutions. They also seem to have been skilled at communicating the meaning of their architecture. For such a small firm, they stand out—even from an international perspective—for having successfully realized so many projects.

Tellus Nursery School, Stockholm 2007–10, facade study.

To give an idea of their skill in this regard, we can look at a recently published review of their Tellus Nursery School (2010). The architect and critic Mikael Bergquist appraised the building in the context of a Swedish construction industry often seen as dictating conditions that make good architecture hard to achieve.[66] He wrote that Tellus, which is a normal public nursery school built and operated on a normal budget, gives "proof that it is [still] possible to create really good architecture" if you challenge "preconceived notions" and embrace the "actual conditions."[67] For Tham & Videgård's very first projects, those conditions were quite limited. In several cases they sought inspiration in Sweden's vernacular building traditions.[68] In an early document they describe how the firm's idea is "to find a contemporary expression for today's needs and desires with a strong foundation in the Swedish vernacular." At the same time they speak of "resonating with current international developments." The short text makes reference both to the rational and simple and to the richly varied.[69] From the beginning Tham & Videgård seemed to be trying to unite simplicity and clarity of conception with a straightforward approach that could nevertheless generate complexity, contrast, and layers of space. In their openness to both contemporary and traditional influences, they seem to have had an inclusive attitude that is independent of convention.

See pages 168–169.

One of their projects with clear Swedish roots is the *Karlsson House*. The building's structure, form, and cladding all play on the building traditions of a nation of scarce resources. By returning to the tradition of board roofing, common until ceramic tile roofing began to dominate in the nineteenth century, the architects could accentuate the coherent solidity of the building volume. At the same time, the simple exterior form encloses a complex interior with varying movements, spatial volumes, and daylighting conditions that all have rather more to do with international architecture. For example, the architects have called one exterior manifestation of this interior complexity, the plank grill hatches over the windows and skylights, "brise-soleil" in a nod to Le Corbusier.[70] It's a reference to an architect whose work was a choreography of movement, a play of surfaces, volumes, and light on the inside and outside of a building. Tham & Videgård have also made direct reference to Le Corbusier regarding their work with transparency.[71] In the case of the Karlsson

House, the exterior is a surface of simplicity and clarity pierced by an interaction between inside and out that is characterized by complexity.

See pages 29–41.

Another building that reveals layered associations is the *Archipelago House*, a work with a strong relationship to the natural landscape that surrounds it. Compared with many of Tham & Videgård's other buildings, this one has no clearly legible mass, but its articulation of the relationship between outdoor spaces and a varied sequence of interior rooms is all the more pronounced. The term "brise-soleil" is actually much more applicable in this home, with its deck pergola and freestanding panel screen wall. The lightweight structure, hovering over the ground on piers, also recalls the Farnsworth House, with its deck and its glass wall folded at right angles. Though obviously more humble in terms of cost, the Archipelago House is nevertheless more wide-ranging and varied in its expression. Tham & Videgård have often remarked on their interest in not treating a building's shell as a definitive boundary; in this case they have given it a kind of fringed transparency.

One project that illustrates the firm's work with contrast and complexity is Snowcrash. It builds in part on Swedish structuralism, with a fixed service core surrounded by a free-flowing work area that can be spatially reordered at will. There are also connections to some of Tham & Videgård's other work. Snowcrash's dark, turbine-like core is surrounded by semitransparent glass walls that make the transition into the brightly lit office space. In Söderöra, instead, the white-painted, top-lit core is enclosed in a solid black shell. The colors are reversed, but in both cases there is a kind of centrifugal acceleration through a fan-blade spatial structure out into the free space that surrounds it. Snowcrash is also similar to Emergency Architecture, their design for refugee camps, in that both erect a mobile architecture around a fixed center—glass in one case, fabric in the other.

Tham & Videgård have described how their initial concepts are often without form, and how form and material are generated from the intrinsic logic and conditions of the project. It is clear from their work that they often elaborate themes, structures, and elements inherited from earlier designs. They have referred to such tools as "architecture's active elements."[72] Without necessarily relying on the architects' own understanding of those elements, it would be worthwhile to explore this aspect of their work a little more closely.

Tham & Videgård have taken an inquisitive, experimental approach to the issue of space and how to order it. In several projects, such as the Kalmar Museum of Art or the Stockholm Concert Hall, a somewhat unconventional view of space planning has led to victory in competitions and parallel commissions. Many of their projects, including Double House, Archipelago House, and Södertälje Tower, are in part characterized by a distinctive treatment of the connection between one space and another. In the Humlegården apartment, they apply a color scheme that articulates a spatial organization that overlaps and expressly differs from the one defined by the walls and doorways.

See page 6.

The building's organization—or major elements of it—is often expressed outwardly in strong geometric forms. Their proposal for *Turku Public Library* had a clear layout and a straightforward circulation pattern neatly contained in a perfect square. Since then the architects have continued to explore the possibilities of basic geometric forms—squares, triangles, pentagons, hexagons. Most remarkable, at least in its Swedish context, is their use of rounded forms and circular plans. Here we can cite the early example of their proposed biology laboratory in New England, where the soft, curvilinear form was both an adaptation to the surrounding landscape and a way to give the rationally ordered interior a richer spatial environment. They based their competition proposal for the Royal Theater in Copenhagen on a circle, a form they also used at a smaller scale for a summerhouse on the island of Vindö. An early built example is the pair of cylindrical duplexes in Lidingö, or the rounded forms of the cloud-shaped glass display case they designed for the Gateau bakery in 2004. Still, the most striking example is probably their almost monumental newly opened yellow building for the Tellus Nursery School on Telefonplan in Stockholm. And in

Summerhouse Vindö 2007, plan.

the archives of preliminary studies for other projects we can find further examples of rounded compositions of three interlinked forms that create a small entrance court between them.[73]

Another important aspect of Tham & Videgård's work is color. Some of the firm's work stands out and is identifiable for its bright colors alone. Nevertheless, it's clear that their use of color is not based on some ideology or psychological theory. They have said they see color as an effective and simple means to achieve various kinds of architectural qualities—and that it is one tool among many others. The same could surely be said of their use of geometric forms.

From their very first commissions, the firm has shown a great interest in the special qualities that fine craftsmanship has given buildings throughout history. Their cafe pavilion in Stureplan and the Karlsson House are two early examples of their effort to create similar qualities using today's industrialized construction methods. Others include their facade systems for the Kalmar Museum of Art, Tellus Nursery School, and the Västra Kajen apartment buildings. For the interior of the apartment in Humlegården they chose to build their design around the hardwood flooring pattern. The ash pieces are manufactured by machine, but they have been tinted with different colors and placed artfully by hand. For the architects, this was a way of playing off the finely wrought detailing of the apartment's original interior. Similarly, the sheet metal surfaces of their Stureplan pavilion and the Moderna Museet Malmö have been cut using sophisticated industrial processes, but the result of their careful treatment at a small scale resonates with the handmade decorative finishes on the buildings that surround them.

Moderna Museet Malmö, 2008–09, interior.

These examples show how often Tham & Videgård's work is characterized by the interplay between two different scales. On the one hand, the building as a whole is often a clear, distilled form wrapped in a single uniform material. On the other hand, the surface of that material is often articulated with subtle nuance and detail. In their work on the museum in Malmö, they said they were trying to avoid the "intermediate scale," and it's clear that approach has been applied to several of their other buildings.[74] For a more in-depth view of Tham & Videgård's work with these design elements, it is worth noting their relationship to art. Since they were students they have been following the contemporary art scene. This interest in art was one of the reasons they decided to participate in the competition in Kalmar, and we can assume that it contributed to many of their scheme's qualities. That success led to the commission to design the Malmö branch of Moderna Museet, where again their experience of art must surely have influenced their design. In any case, the realization of the two museums has given Tham & Videgård a unique position. It would be hard to name another Swedish architect in the postwar period who has designed two such important art museums in such a short span of time, and in so doing garnered so much attention.

We can find traces of their interest in art in other aspects of their work as well. They have noted, for example, how the artist Anselm Kiefer alters the expression of an object by reproducing it in an unexpected material, as in his famous sculptures of airplanes made of lead. It is clear that Tham & Videgård have been interested in how such phenomena can transform and charge a work of architecture. They most often attempt the feat in their treatment of a building's facade and roof. In fact, several projects show them treating a building in the abstract terms of surface and volume rather than as a collection of structural components such as roof, facade, or base. As in Kiefer's sculptures, this is a straightforward way to give the building a charged expression.[75]

For Tham & Videgård, art has provided a basis for fundamental observations of how space design, material choice and treatment, light effects, and contrasting scales can alter and strengthen the impact of a work of architecture. For example, it's possible to see a relationship between art and their work with color and geometry. One project worth noting in this regard is their interior design for the Museum of Far Eastern Antiquities in Stockholm, yet another competition win. There the architects

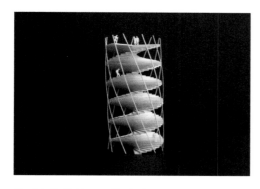

Double Helix Tower, Barkarby,
Invited competition, 1st prize, 2011.

created what they call a "hovering golden dragon"—a consolidated prismatic volume of display cases that floats in the middle of a gallery. The drawn-out, "golden," geometrically folded form glimmering in a black space can bring to mind the spatial pieces by Yayoi Kusama, another artist to whom Tham & Videgård have made reference. The contrast between a shimmering object and the dark void that surrounds it creates a dream-like space. An example of another kind of spatial connection to art is their early competition proposal for a New England biology laboratory. The long, curvilinear building, with its facade of double green silk-screened glass undulating through the surrounding landscape, was informed by the Land Art movement of the American sixties and seventies.[76]

Another illustrative example of the influence of art on Tham & Videgård's work is their Humlegården apartment renovation. The finished design could almost be called an art installation, though that wasn't the architects' intention or objective. They have added a new spatial order layered on top of the apartment's original layout by tinting the parquet flooring in the varied hues of autumn leaves. These colors have also been wrapped up the walls as wainscoting, doorframes, bookcases, and kitchen cabinets. The apartment conveys the feeling of a leaf-strewn forest floor, the individual components of the interior millwork buried in color. The walls themselves, however, are painted white. The effect of the contrast between the white and the bright colors is heightened by the fact that all of the loose furniture in the apartment is white. According to the architects, the idea with the white paint is to neutralize the objects with regard to their ages and make it easier to compare them as pure objects or constructions.[77] At the same time, we could also see this as an artistic strategy. We might refer, for example, to the work of another artist cited by the architects: Rosemarie Trockel's *Hot Plate*. That piece can be read as an example of how changing the context of an everyday object can charge it with a different significance. The furniture pieces in the Humlegården apartment have in fact lost some of their personal and familiar character, and have become distanced from us, like strangers. Combining this visually gripping atmosphere with the apartment's utilitarian domestic function raises basic questions about the home, its character, and its contents in just the way art can lead us to see the world in a different light.

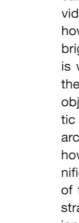

Martin Videgård and Bolle Tham, Beijing 2009.

As we have seen, Tham & Videgård launched their office with the explicit intention of basing their work on the Swedish vernacular. At the same time, they have embraced contemporary architecture as part of the global context. Though they have never stated so in formal descriptions of their work, it is evident that an important aspect of their architectural thinking is related to their interest in art and its explorations. Their commitment to reality has not been limited to working within the practical constraints of a project or their efforts to get their projects built; it has also been about experimenting with reality, with the experience of the world. In so doing they have manifested a duality in their work, embracing what comes out of the real but also what comes out of the imagination.

In their practice, Tham & Videgård explore this duality through reinterpretations or displacements that give a distinctive charge to what is otherwise in many respects quite pragmatic work. They manage to create simplicity animated by rich expression—a straightforward and down-to-earth architecture that still vibrates with imaginative energy in relation to the real world. An interlacing of clarity and complexity that will continue to inform their work as it develops into the future.

/ JL

[1] The original name of the firm was Tham Videgård Hansson Arkitekter AB, after some years written Tham & Videgård Hansson Arkitekter AB. In 2009, Martin Videgård Hansson simplified his surname by dropping the Hansson, and they changed their name to Tham & Videgård Arkitekter (T&V). Unless otherwise noted, factual information in this book has been taken from the office's own digital archives (TVA) and from recurring conversations with representatives of the office during 2010 and 2011. Where no other source is given, my characterization of Tham & Videgård's positions and ideas stems from these conversations.

[2] The way they relate to Swedish tradition is a recurring theme in reviews of their work. Peter Cook commends them for "clearly knowing their heritage" and also for the fact Tham & Videgård "have broken the dreaded Swedish spell." This relationship is also treated, in different ways, in both essays in the first book about Tham & Videgård. Peter Cook, "Tham & Videgård," *Let's Talk About Houses: Between the North and the South*. Lisbon Architecture Triennale, 2010; Hans Ibelings, "Just Architecture," and Kieran Long, "The Tower of Babel," Tomas Lauri (ed), *Tham & Videgård Arkitekter*, Arvinius förlag, Stockholm, 2009.

[3] Relatively few Swedish architecture firms are regularly acknowledged in the international architectural press and professional publications. T&V are among them. For empirical substantiation, though from the kind of source that can never be entirely accurate, we can note Baunetz's rankings of published projects: in Nov/Dec 2010 T&V topped all Swedish firms in 78th place overall. http://www.baunetz.de/ranking/, accessed 5 Feb 2011.

[4] The award was established by Svenska Arkitektföreningen (now the Swedish Association of Architects) in 1962 on a donation from the former Stockholm City Architect Kasper Salin. It was first given to the almost eighty-year-old Sigurd Lewerentz for his St. Mark's Church in Skarpnäck (outside Stockholm). T&V are among very few firms to receive the honor during the first decade of their practice.

[5] Claes Caldenby, "Vid medelvägen slut? 1975–98," Caldenby (ed.), *1900-talets svenska arkitektur. Att bygga ett land* (20th Century Swedish Architecture: Building a Country). Arkitekturmuseet, Stockholm, 1998.

[6] A more thorough presentation of the architects' education may be found in the biographies below.

[7] The competition was won by the Finnish firm of JKMM, founded in 1998.

[8] Tham and Videgård have said that they have a "strong shared viewpoint" and that their ongoing conversation is intuitive. See Lauri's interview with the architects in *Tham & Videgård Arkitekter*, 2009, p 5.

[9] Claes Caldenby, (ed.), *Arkitektur i förändring* (Architecture in Transition): *A4, ELLT, Coordinator 1954–91*. Svensk byggtjänst, Stockholm, 2000, p 12.

[10] Sven Backström, Leif Reinius, Eva Rudberg, "Att berika funktionalismen" (Enriching Functionalism), interview in *Arkitektur*, 6 (1982).

[11] It is worth noting that the firm's founders executed a number of minor projects together before the office was officially established. T&V's list of works includes notes from as early as 1996–97 about work on an installation and interior design for part of Operakällaren (the Royal Opera House restaurant) in collaboration with the artist Leif Elgren. For the year 1997 there are references to the set design for a fashion show at NK department store, and in 1998 they completed a number of minor cafe and restaurant interiors. TVA.

[12] Memo dated 12 Nov 1999. TVA.

[13] Interview with T&V, fall 2010. See also Daniel Golling, Bolle Tham, Martin Videgård, "Bolle & Martin" [interview], *Rum*, 4 (2001).

[14] There is a preliminary description of the site and program dated 6 Dec 1999. Memo by Tham & Videgård dated 8 Nov 2000 in letter by Bolle Tham to the Department of Planning and Buildings, Upplands-Bro, 8 Nov 2000.

[15] Bolle Tham, letter to the Department of Planning and Buildings, Upplands-Bro, 8 Nov 2000.

[16] Preliminary concept for Ugglero House dated 6 Dec 1999. TVA.

[17] Bengt Lindroos, *Ur den svenska byggnadskonstens magasin*. Arkitektur, Stockholm, 1989.

[18] Nina Gunne, "Enkla lösningar höll nere priset" (Simple Solutions Kept Costs Low), interview published in a marketing flyer from the Swedish Association of Architects distributed with the newspaper *Dagens Nyheter*, 9 Sept 2003.

[19] The award was established by the The Advertising Association of Sweden. In its first year, it received about two hundred submissions from ten different countries. The submissions were reviewed by a jury that included Alberto Meda, Dieter Rams, and Gert Wingårdh. *CoreDesign 2001*. The Advertising Association of Sweden, Stockholm, 2002.

[20] Karin Löfgren, "Snowcrash, Stockholm," *Arkitektur*, 1 (2002). Tomas Lauri, "Snowcrash," *Forum*, 1 (2002); Tomas Lauri, "Tio-i-topp 2001, introduktion," *Forum*, 1 (2002). In *Forum* the project was presented as a nominee for the best interior designs of 2001, an honor bestowed on ten of the fifty-three projects submitted for consideration.

[21] For example: "100 Tage design," *Architektur*, 1 (2003); Beppe Finessi, "Snowcrash," *Rivista Abitare*, 421 (2002); Snowcrash, "Snowcrash, 101 Day Office," *Spaces*, 1 (2002); Ana Varea, "Oficinas Snowcrash en Estocolmo (Suecia)," *Constructiva*, 14 (2003).

[22] Klas Tham already had experience with a number of important urban planning projects. As a partner in Arken Architects he had been responsible for a major mixed 100,000 m² development in Skarpnäck, Stockholm, the first block of which won the Kasper Salin Prize in 1983. Between 1995 and 2001 he worked as the principal exhibition architect for the European housing expo Bo01 held in Malmö during the summer of 2001 — one of Sweden's most important housing expos since H55 (Helsingborg, 1955). For Bo01 he was responsible for the program and the design of the master plan for permanent residential and commercial development, which totals over 200,000 square meters.

[23] Another long and narrow single-family home from the same period is Blom House. There too the architects created an interplay of room volumes woven together across two levels of expanding and contracting space.

[24] The characterization of the home as a "three-dimensional puzzle" was used by Tham & Videgård themselves in a page on their Web site created 9 Aug 2006. It is worth noting that the same work with spatial variations described here recurs in Blom House. TVA.

[25] The competition began 26 Aug and ended 1 Dec 2004, and 294 submissions were received. *Konstmuseum i Kalmar: allmän arkitekttävling 2004: juryns utlåtande 2005-02-02*. Handout Kalmar kommun, 2005.

[26] Bolle Tham, Martin Videgård Hansson, "House K, Stocksund," *Arkitektur*, 1 (2005), p 10.

[27] Tham & Videgård did develop one scheme with a lower building before deciding to build vertically.

[28] Lauri, Tham, Videgård, "Intervju," 2009, pp 6–7.

[29] Work on the renovation of House Z began in 2000. The design was based on a movement between levels staggered down a steep slope. Tham & Videgård described the project as "A private house treated as part of a terraced garden." "House Z i Danderyd," Web site document created Dec 18, 2003, TVA.

[30] The cost of construction was about 20,500 SEK per square meter (about 2,350€/m²).

[31] Ten residents of Kalmar appealed the zoning plan for the museum all the way to the Swedish Supreme Administrative Court. Ulrika Widell, "Klart för nytt museum i stadsparken," *Barometern*, 3 July 2007.

[32] The building was shortlisted in 2008 at the World Architecture Festival in Barcelona. The following year it became the first Swedish building ever shortlisted for the Mies van der Rohe Award.

[33] The reference appears for the first time in the jury's statement and is later repeated frequently, though never by the architects themselves; instead they cite Klas Anshelm as a Swedish source of inspiration. *Konstmuseum i Kalmar: allmän arkitekttävling 2004: juryns utlåtande 2005-02-02*. Handout, Kalmar kommun, 2005; *Arkitektur*, 4 (2008); Fredric Bedoire, "Kalmar konstmuseum," in Mark Irving & Fredric Bedoire (ed.), *1001 byggnader du måste se innan du dör*, Bonnier fakta, Stockholm, 2009.

[34] *Kalmar konstmuseum*. Competition entry, Tham & Videgård. TVA.

[35] Bolle Tham, Martin Videgård Hansson, "Nya Kalmar," *Arkitektur*, 1 (2005), p 10.

[36] *Planbeskrivning P02016: Detaljplan för Glasberga Gård*. Adopted 17 Feb 2004 by the Community Planning Board, Södertälje.

[37] They used a similar scheme in a plan for the island of Styrsö, outside Gothenburg, which they were working on at the same time. A variation on the gable theme also recurs in plans for Linnaeus University in Kalmar from 2009.

[38] A study by Tham & Videgård dated 10 Oct 2006 refers to urban space in the towns of Eksjö, Falun, Linköping, and Smögen.

[39] *Entré till KTH-campus och arkitekturskola. Utvärdering av parallella uppdrag juli 2007.* Handout, Akademiska Hus & KTH, 2007.

[40] The project is treated further below under the heading "Architecture and the Reality of Learning: An Ongoing Project."

[41] The other firms invited to compete were: Erséus Arkitekter, Semrén & Månsson Arkitektkontor, Kanozi arkitekter, Kjellander + Sjöberg arkitektkontor.

[42] *Juryutlåtande: Inbjuden projekttävling för Västra Kajen, Jönköping*. Handout, VätterHem & Riksbyggen, 2009.

[43] In the competition proposal, this outer facade layer was a wooden lattice, though they are currently exploring other material options.

[44] The other participating firms were Tengbom arkitekter and AIX arkitekter. The City of Södertälje has still not decided whether to go forward with the project or not.

[45] *Program för parallellt uppdrag: kv. Garvaren, Södertälje: 2007-09-12.* Handout, Sweco FFNS, Telge Fastigheter, City of Södertälje, 2007.

[46] *Parallellt uppdrag—Kv. Garvaren 2007-11-23.* Competition entry, Tham & Videgård. TVA.

[47] The other invited firms were BIG, 3xN, and Wingårdhs. The invitation from Sveafastigheter and the City of Stockholm is dated 15 March 2010.

[48] *Vällingby Parkstad: Program för detaljplan för Vattenfallet 2.* Handout, City of Stockholm, Sveafastigheter, Gillberg arkitekter, 2009.

[49] *Vällingby parkstad—Entrébyggnad.* Tham & Videgård, 2010. The final presentation was made 14 May 2010. TVA.

[50] *Vällingby parkstad—Entrébyggnad.* Competition entry, Tham & Videgård, 2010. TVA.

[51] One mock-up for the presentation includes a photograph of the space beneath the Eiffel Tower shown both right-side up and upside down. The mock-up is dated 13 May 2010. TVA.

[52] *Urban emergency nodes.* Project description dated 30 May 2009. Tham & Videgård. TVA. See also the catalogue *Crossing: Dialogues for Emergency Architecture.* National Art Museum of China, Beijing, 2009.

[53] Tham & Videgård did end up playing a role in the competition: in the spring of 2007 they designed the exhibition of the five finalists for the Swedish Museum of Architecture in Stockholm.

[54] They have even designed homes for Arkitekthus, a prefab homebuilder whose models are all designed by some of the most renown architects in Sweden. Since 2006, a number of different versions of Tham & Videgård's designs have been built.

[55] There is also a connection between this simple Swedish vacation cottage and Andrea Palladio's classic Villa Rotonda. Apart from their obvious differences, both consist of a lofty central space that is top-lit from a lantern or skylight and surrounded by porticoes that face each of the cardinal directions. For further commentary on this comparison, see Johan Linton, Martin Videgård Hansson, Bolle Tham, "Arkitekturen och det generella," *Psykoanalytisk Tid/Skrift*, 24–25 (2008).

[56] A mock-up of the presentation for Vällingby Parkstad was titled "Trädkoja Vällingby" (Vällingby Tree House). The document is dated 15 May 2010. TVA.

[57] Looking back at the firm's early concepts for the Stureplan project, we find in fact descriptions of not just a box, but "a compact red box." Gateau Stureplan, memo dated 12 Nov 1999, TVA. The connection to the pavilion on Stureplan has been made in reviews of the museum. Olof Hultin, "En säker tonträff," *Arkitektur*, 1 (2010).

[58] Digital sketch created 3 Feb 2009. TVA.

[59] Tham & Videgård were invited to participate in June 2009, and the first meeting was held that September. The other invited firms were AIX arkitekter, Tengbom arkitekter, and White arkitekter. In May 2010 Tham & Videgård were notified that they had been chosen to continue the planning of the building. TVA.

[60] Anders Bergström, *Arkitekten Ivar Tengbom: byggnadskonst på klassisk grund*. Diss. KTH, Stockholm. Byggförlaget, Stockholm, 2001, pp 158–75.

[61] AIX arkitekter also suggested the possibility of building on the existing roof, though they chose to pursue another scheme in their proposal. *Konserthuset: Parallellt uppdrag 2009-11-17.* Competition entry, Tham & Videgård, 2009; *Konserthuset: Etapp 7*, Competition entry, AIX, 2009. TVA.

[62] The other firms were AIX arkitekter, Marge arkitekter, and Visby arkitektgrupp. The invitation came in January 2010.

[63] *Juryutlåtanden för inbjuden arkitekttävling för Bergmancenter på Fårö*, 2010.

[64] *Bergmancenter på Fårö*, Handout, 2010. Competition entry, Tham & Videgård, 2010, TVA.

[65] Claes Caldenby, "Vid medelvägens slut? 1975–98," in Caldenby (ed.), *1900-talets svenska arkitektur. Att bygga ett land*. Swedish Museum of Architecture, Stockholm, 1998.

[66] Mikael Bergquist has published writings about architecture in Sweden and abroad for two decades. Since 1996, he has interviewed a large number of different architects and theorist for *Arkitektur* (The Swedish Review of Architecture), for example Tony Fretton, Wilfried Wang, Moussavi Farshid, Peter Märkli, and Coop Himmelb(l)au.

[67] Mikael Bergquist, "Begränsningar med storartade effekter," *Arkitektur*, 8 (2010).

[68] This fascination with the simplicity of the Swedish vernacular was already prominent in the architecture program at KTH in the late 19th century, and has been a recurring feature of Swedish architecture ever since.

[69] "Tham Videgård Hansson Arkitekter," document created 7 May 2002. TVA.

[70] As the firm's press material from the recent years acknowledges. TVA.

[71] The concept of transparency as it is interpreted in Colin Rowe's and Robert Slutzky's famous essay published in two parts in *Perspecta* 1963 and 1971. See Lauri, Tham, Videgård, "Intervju," 2009, p 7.

[72] Lauri, Tham, Videgård, "Intervju," 2009, p 8.

[73] For example, in a preliminary study for the Brick House.

[74] Bolle Tham, Martin Videgård, "Moderna Museet Malmö," *Arkitektur*, 1 (2010). In this connection Tham and Videgård has referred to an article by the former dean at KTH: Staffan Henriksson, "En riktig Juvel" (A real Jewel), *Mama*, 7 (1994).

[75] Other artists they have named as sources of such inspiration include Rachel Whitread, Anish Kapoor, and the Swedish artist Fredrik Wretman.

[76] One could also mention the widely publicized Tree Hotel in Harads, that explores similar phenomenas as in the works of Dan Graham and Robert Morris (in a specific reference, they have named Robert Morris's work *Untitled [Mirrored Cubes],* 1965/1971). In addition, their design for Vällingby Parkstad bear a resemblance to works by Eduardo Chillida and Jorge Oteiza, some of which appear as reference material in the project folders. TVA.

[77] In another context Tham and Videgård have told that when they are out travelling they usually imagine the studied buildings as white, "to reset our vision and perceive them from a different perspective." Lauri, Tham, Videgård, "Intervju," 2009, p 13.

Works

Archipelago House
2003–06

In 2003, Tham & Videgård began work on a summerhouse in the outer archipel-ago outside Stockholm. Their objective was to use the dramatic landscape to cre-ate a kind of framework, or platform, for various interpretations of the relationship between building and nature. The form of the plan comes from the specific char-acteristics of the lot, the building fit carefully between two outcroppings of bedrock and turned to face the sun to the south and the water to the west. The sprawling, lightweight structure of wood and glass resonates with both the broad horizon and the tall pines that surround it. Their design is also influenced by the fact that all of the construction materials needed to be transported to the site by boat.

Inside, a series of rambling social spaces spreads out along a wide-open terrace. These interior and exterior zones are divided (and joined) by a zigzag glass screen with sliding doors. On the back side of the living areas lie bedrooms and utility spaces. The changing directions of the glass screen help to vary the views and to create corners of wind-sheltered outdoor space. The detailing of the wood-panel facade, with a black stain that lets the building blend in among the tall, dark pines, underscores the building's lightness and transparency. With its pergola roof that dif-fuses direct sunlight, the terrace dissolves the boundary between inside and out. The interior is painted white, and interior furnishings such as the closets and beds were made on site and built in.

Archipelago House
2003–06

3

1   Terrace screen of stained pine plywood.
2   The sprawling glass facade corresponds to the horizon of the sea to
     the west.

3   The pergola of wooden joists filters the light of the sky and defines
     the space of the terrace. Together with the terrace screen, it creates a
     moving pattern of light and shadow.
4   The terrace is a transition space between the interior of the home
     and the surrounding natural environment.
5   Facade and pergola details.

6   Evening view from the south. Sliding glass doors make it possible to
     move freely between indoor and outdoor spaces. There are two in
     each section of the folded glass. The glass is oriented to frame views of
     the water, while the long diagonal aligns with the primary axis of
     the sun.

7 *Living room interior. The floor and doors are of white-glazed white oak, and the walls are white-painted tongue-and-groove boarding.*

8 *Interior of guest bedroom with built-in bunk beds.*

9 *Interior of master bedroom open to the terrace and the view of the Baltic Sea.*

8

10

11

10   Children's bedroom with built-in bunk beds and storage shelves.
11   Kitchen interior.

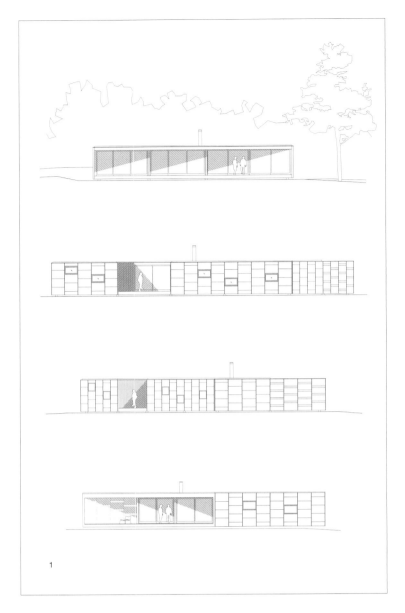

1

2

3

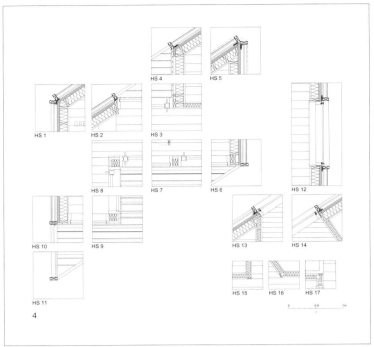

4

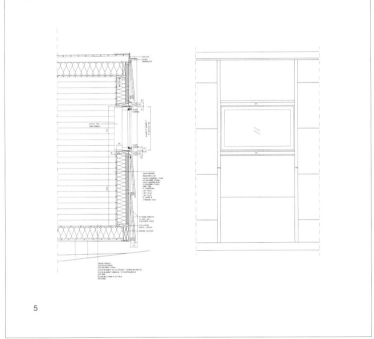

5

1   Elevations.
2   Plan. The diagonal shifting of the rooms reflects adapting
     to the specifics of the site.
3   Section.
4   Details, horizontal sections.
5   Details, vertical section and facade.
6   Satellite photo of the site in Stockholm's outer archipelago.
7–8 Presentation model made of wood, essentially identical
     to the house as built.
9   Guest cottage foundation.
10–11 Images from the construction site.

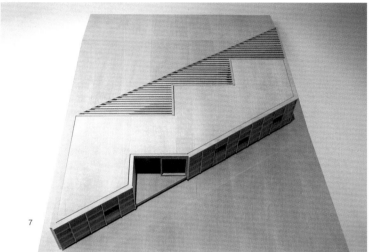

Design team: Tove Belfrage, Lukas Thiel, Bolle Tham, Martin Videgård.

Tellus Nursery School
2007–10

The ongoing transformation of Ericsson's former industrial area on Telefonplan in Stockholm to a residential neighborhood has created a demand for more nursery schools. Tham & Videgård were commissioned by the city to design one for a narrow lot located where the old industrial zone abuts a wooded area. One important objective was for the building to negotiate the transition from the large-scale environment of the forest and the industrial and office buildings to the smaller and more concentrated places of the new community.

In order to mediate between the different spatial scales, they created an outdoor entrance court as a kind of buffer. The architects designed the space as a half-open courtyard, a place for children and parents to gather before or after school. They used curvilinear forms to encourage movement and generate both interior and exterior spaces with a distinctive character.

Tham & Videgård developed the floor plan in collaboration with the school staff. The organization of spaces is therefore influenced by the school's Reggio Emilia educational philosophy. Each of the six groups of children has its own separate space for gathering, quiet play, and rest. These spaces adjoin a large, continuous central space for activities and project stations where the groups can play together around various themes. The windows are set freely at different heights, with the intention of adapting the daylighting and views to the children and facilitating their contact with the play space in the courtyard and the surrounding forest. The interior has been given bold colors: pink, yellow, blue, and green zones correspond to the spatial organization. The largest spaces can be divided into smaller rooms with the help of draperies.

The exterior facade is board-and-batten siding that is painted bright yellow and wrapped around the curves of the building. By letting the battens continue across some of the windows, the architects have underscored the building's arcing contours and modulated the direct sunlight inside. The building's frame is concrete cast on site using insulation board as concrete forms, a strategy that has helped meet the high standards of environmental sensitivity and energy conservation demanded of every aspect of the project.

Tellus Nursery School
2007–10

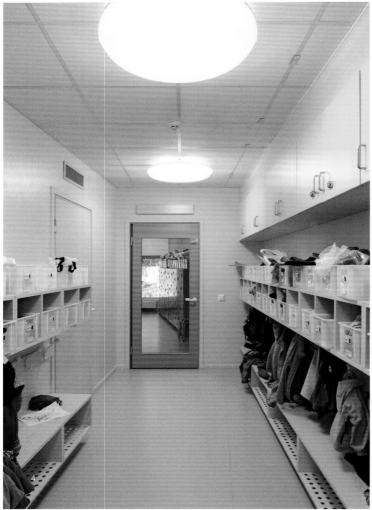

1   *Courtyard with entrance. The screen roof over the entrance is a solid sheet of steel.*

2   *In the courtyard, looking up to the sky. In some places the painted pine ribs continue uninterrupted over the outside of the window openings.*

3–5   *Dining room, coat room, and group room. The colors underscore the articulation of each space and structure the layout.*

5

6

6   *South elevation in evening light.*

7–8   *Exterior and courtyard facades at dusk. In the evening, the colorful interiors contribute to color variations on the outside as well.*

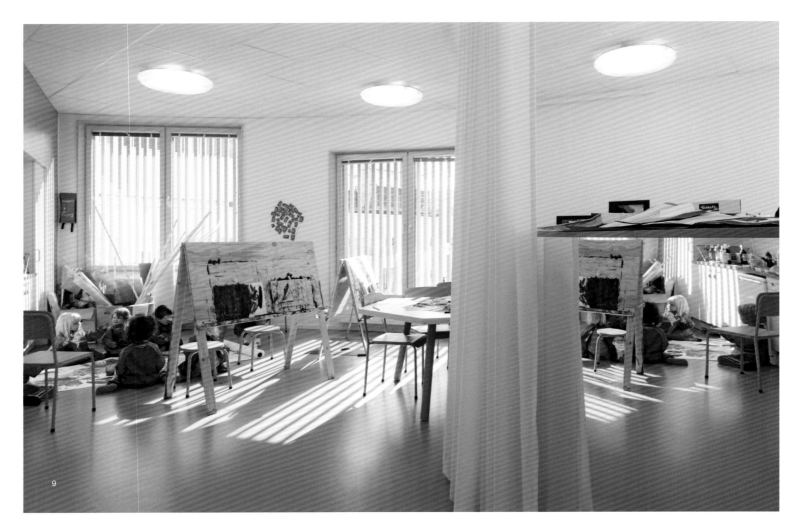

9,11   *"Plaza" with various activity stations. The size and shape of the rooms can be varied using draperies. The plan is designed to allow the arrangement of furniture to change over time. The space is intentionally vaguely articulated to encourage it to be used more freely.*

10   *The passage into the entrance courtyard.*

12   *Courtyard viewed from the upper level. The windows are installed at varying elevations as though to accommodate children of every size.*

11

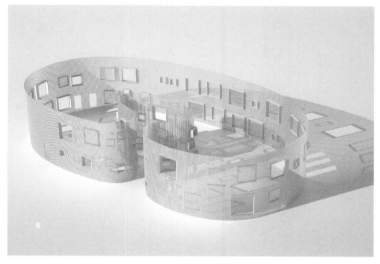

1   Site plan.
2   Plans and elevations.
3   The building section shows the tension between the industrial area and the forest.
4   Construction details.
5   Aerial view.
6   Facade study.
7–9 Construction site photos. The concrete walls were cast on site into insulated concrete forms, combining the tasks of building forms and installing insulation into a single operation. The floors are cast concrete as well.

Design team: Eric Engström, Mårten Nettelbladt, Andreas Helgesson, Johan Björkholm, Karolina Nyström, Marcus Andrén, Anna Katharina Koss, Bolle Tham, Martin Videgård.

Landscape architects: Nyréns landskap / Bengt Isling.

Kalmar Museum of Art
2004–08

Tham & Videgård were awarded the commission to design Kalmar Konstmuseum after winning first prize in an open international architectural competition in 2004. The museum needed a new building for its growing collection of modern art, temporary exhibitions, and various public events. The location in historic Kalmar's city park was charged with significance. Besides its proximity to Kalmar Castle (one of only a few monumental buildings in Sweden from the Renaissance), the museum was to adjoin the little Byttan restaurant (1939), one of Swedish modernist architect Sven-Ivar Lind's most important works. The museum was completed on a relatively small budget, and opened in May 2008. It has been awarded the Kasper Salin Prize (Sweden's highest architectural honor) and has been shortlisted for the Mies van der Rohe Award (the European Union Prize for Contemporary Architecture).

The architects' motto for their competition submission was "Platform," a word that summed up its conceptual idea: to design the building as a series of open platforms for a variety of art activities. Tham & Videgård strove to follow that motto spatially and structurally as well. The "platforms" are free-spanning open spaces stacked one on top of another. The resulting building is a tall cubic volume with large glazed openings onto the surrounding park. In contrast to the monumental form of its exterior, the interiors are of a more intimate scale. The intention was to vary the character of the spaces in order to make the building as flexible as possible. The lower gallery space is open to the park along the entire length of one side, and the upper gallery is top-lit through sawtooth skylights that also increase its ceiling height. In addition to staff, mechanical, and service space, the building also includes a public library and workshops.

Entering from the park, a thin canopy roof forms a spatial link that connects the museum to the Byttan restaurant. Inside the entrance, a stair of bare in situ concrete connects the building's four levels in an unbroken square spiral that is lit from above. The concrete formwork for the stair was waxed, which has given its surfaces a sheen and made them soft to the touch. To ascend to the top of the building is to climb up into the treetops above the park. The spatial intensity is accentuated by the use of bold colors on wall paneling and other interior elements.

One of the motivations for the tall building was to minimize its footprint and thereby its intrusion into the relatively limited park grounds—an idea that helped Tham & Videgård win the competition. It also allowed the building to become a vertical extension of the paths through the park. Despite the park's relatively level topography, the museum provides spaces from which visitors can view the city from new perspectives.

The structure is cast-in-place concrete with posttensioned beams. The interior combines exposed concrete with black-stained plywood panels framing doorways and mechanical services. The architects have also designed several pieces of furniture for the interior.

Kalmar Museum of Art
2004–08

1   North and east elevations facing the park. The four-story cube is
    clad in black-stained plywood panels.
2   The second-floor white box gallery—a space for temporary
    exhibitions. The concrete beams are cast in place and designed
    to span the sixteen-meter-long space. Their depth also hides
    much of the mechanical systems.

3   East elevation with the windows of the white box gallery.
4   Winding staircase seen from below: a concrete structure cast in
    place with no expansion joints, which contributes to its solid
    appearance. Two high windows admit light from above that pours
    down through the stairwell.

5   Gallery for the permanent collection. The north-facing windows of
    the sawtooth roof fill the room with the light of a classic artist's studio.

4

6

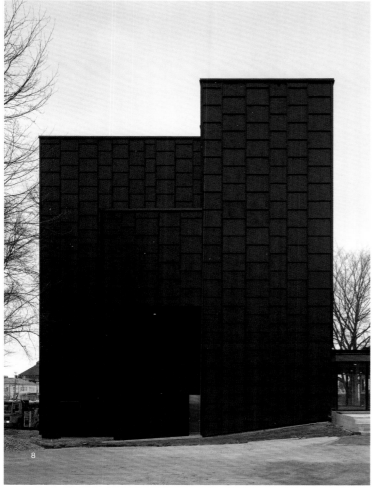

6   *Black-stained pine plywood facade. The facade is designed to play off the branches and leafy canopy of the trees.*

7   *White display case in the permanent collection gallery.*

8   *West elevation. The projecting portion holds the space for video art, and at the same time provides a roof over the loading dock. The red-painted loading area is visible through the open door.*

9   *In the foreground, Sven-Ivar Lind's Byttan Restaurant from 1939. The building is light, horizontal, and oriented to face Kalmar Castle. Behind it, the museum is tall, black, and turned toward the water. The architects' intention was to allow the two to be understood as freestanding buildings that are linked together.*

10

10–12 *The marks of the forms inside the concrete stairwell reflect the pattern on the exterior facades. The concrete walls were cast into waxed pine plywood forms. From the top of the stair there is a view of the castle. The building establishes a new topography, giving the park a new set of views.*

13 *North elevation, showing how the building has been nestled in among the park's tall trees.*

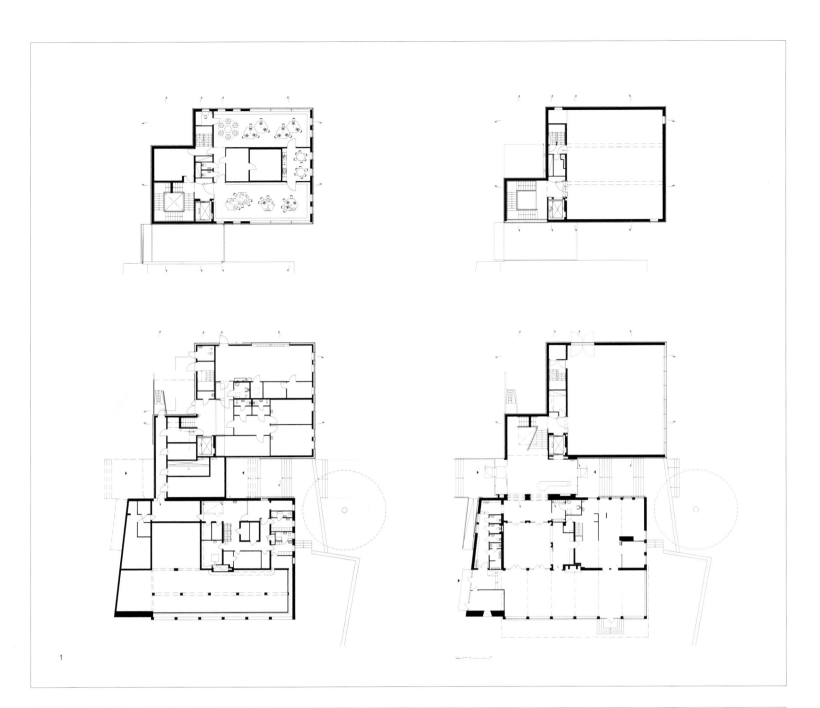

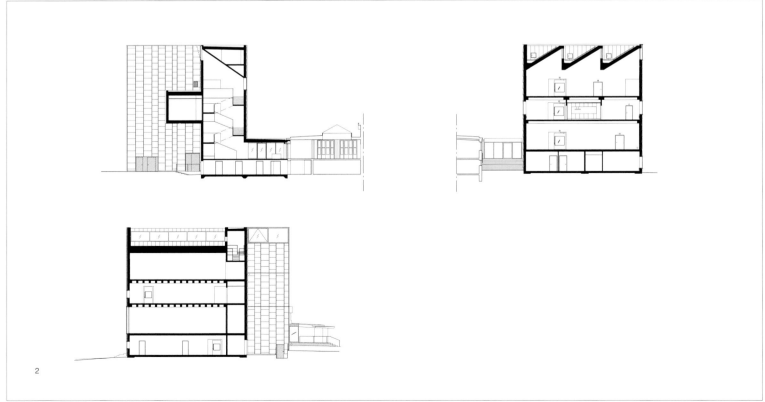

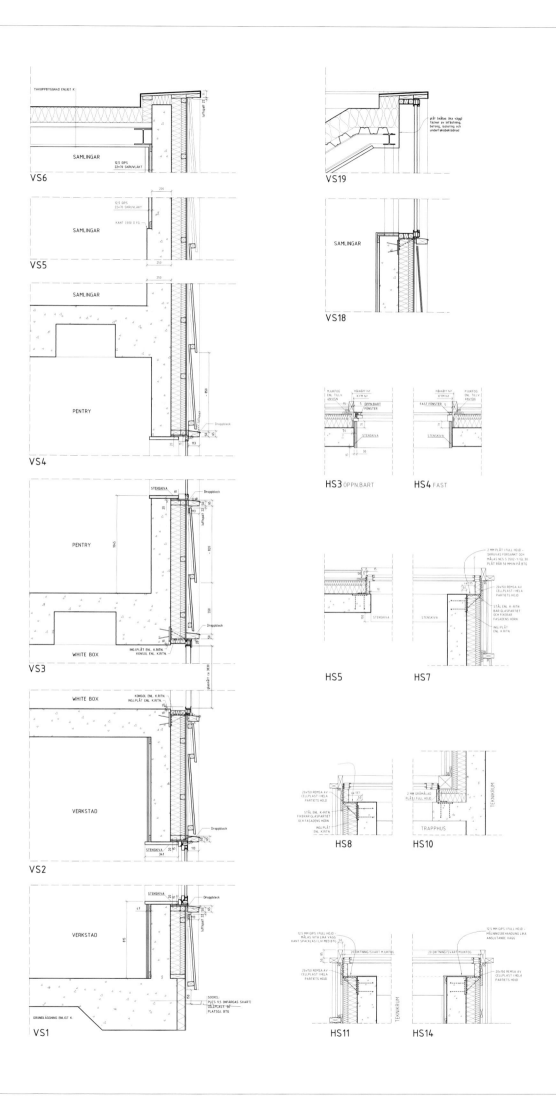

VS6

VS5

VS4

VS3

VS2

VS1

VS19

VS18

HS3 OPPN.BART   HS4 FAST

HS5   HS7

HS8   HS10

HS11   HS14

3

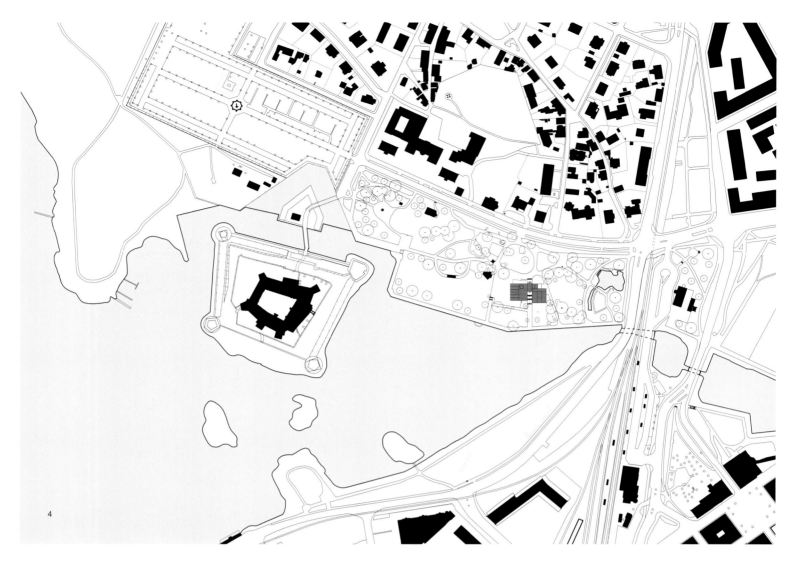

4

1   *Lower ground floor (left) and entrance level with white box (right).*
2   *Second floor (left) with video art gallery, library, and offices; third floor (right) with gallery for permanent collection.*
3   *Building sections.*

4   *Construction detail section through exterior wall.*
5   *Aerial photograph.*
6   *Model.*
7   *Concept section view.*
8–11   *Construction site photos.*

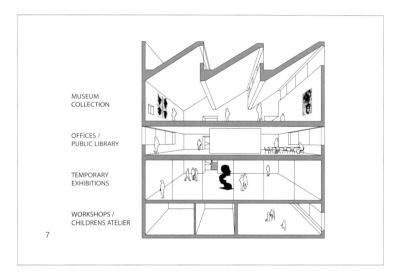

MUSEUM COLLECTION

OFFICES / PUBLIC LIBRARY

TEMPORARY EXHIBITIONS

WORKSHOPS / CHILDRENS ATELIER

Design team: Lukas Thiel, Tove Belfrage, Johan Björkholm, Fredrik Nilsson, Erik Wåhlström, Bolle Tham, Martin Videgård.

Atrium House
2002–10

Atrium House is a vacation home in När Parish on the island of Gotland. It is built on a slight ridge that marks the location of the coastline a thousand years ago—the edge where the land once met the sea.

In the context of this open, expansive landscape, the building seems more like a low wall than a house. It is planned around a completely enclosed atrium courtyard that is designed to serve as a fixed point, a sheltered outdoor room, while the rest of the property is left undisturbed as a meadow where grazing sheep prevent the land from returning to forest.

The house is inspired by the strong materiality of Gotland's vernacular agricultural architecture. Another source of inspiration were the remains of a unique square medieval wooden fortress, known as Bulverket, found in the middle of the island's second-largest lake, Tingstäde Marsh. Like Bulverket, Tham & Videgård's Atrium House is an austere architectural structure in which the elements required for everyday functions have been reduced to a minimum. The house is narrow, but its openings outward are broad, which gives the interior the character of a sheltering niche in the open space of the landscape. While the roof plane maintains a consistent elevation throughout the house, the interior floor steps up and down in accordance with the surrounding terrain. That means the ceiling height varies among the main spaces, which are arranged in a continuous ring around the atrium. The house may be entered from any one of three different openings toward the atrium. The smaller rooms have been consolidated in a number of solid blocks. In winter, the storage room can double as a mudroom.

The large glass panels glide in tracks hung on the surface of the outside walls, according to the same principle as many barn doors. Even the interior doors are surface-mounted, allowing the walls to appear unbroken.

Atrium House
2002–10

3

1   *East elevation viewed from the north. The house lies on the shore of the Baltic Sea, fit between the existing oak and ash trees.*

2   *Living room with fireplace. The floor elevation is lower than the atrium, but coincides with the grade level surrounding the house. The finished floor is the polished surface of the self-compacting concrete slab. The walls are unpigmented lime stucco.*

3   *Dining area overlooking the meadow and sea to the south. The sliding glass panels allow the house to open up onto the farmland that surrounds it. The change in floor elevation is dimensioned to provide seating around the edge of the room.*

4–5   *Grandmother's room. Built-in box bed of waxed pine plywood.*

6   *South elevation, facing the sea in evening light. The walls are rendered in lime stucco pigmented with carbon black, the roof and flashing of oxidized zinc. The surface-mounted sliding glass doors are of tar oiled oak, a preservative treatment that allows the wood to become gray over time in harmony with the other facade materials. The house has the appearance of a low stone wall fit into the landscape.*

7   *Dining room with fireplace.*

8   *The passage between kitchen and dining room.*

8

9

10

11

9 Bedroom with bunk beds. The lower bunk can be expanded to sleep two by placing another bunk on the cleats affixed to the walls. Each bed has its own window niche. With their deeply splayed sides, the small windows still provide plenty of light.

10 South elevation at dusk.

11 View from atrium toward living room.

12 Exterior with windows for (from left to right) kitchen, master bedroom, and workshop.

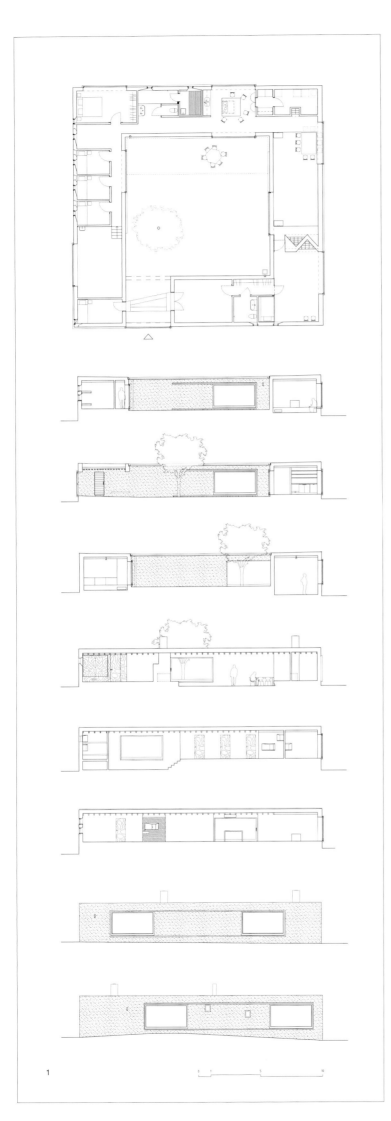

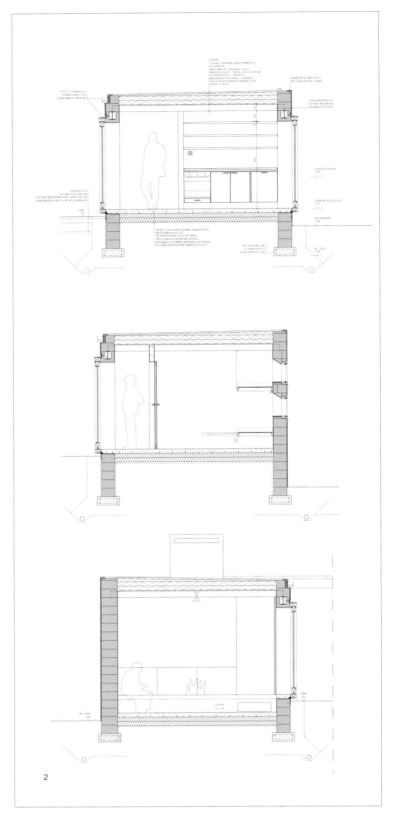

1 Plan, section, elevation.

2 Construction sections. The flat roof structure is designed to leave all organic material exposed on the inside, with only inorganic materials on top. This way the moisture from an eventual leak can evaporate to the interior air.

3 Site.

4 Site model 1:200.

5 Working model 1:100.

6–8 Construction site photos.

9 Atrium patio with concrete pavers, grass, and a magnolia. The entrance passage will be planted with climbing vines.

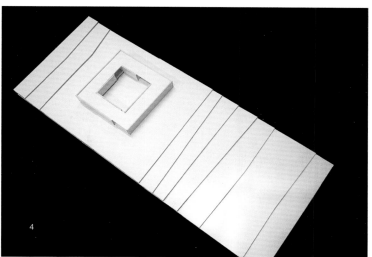

Design team: Bolle Tham, Martin Videgård.

Söderöra
2005–08

The house is located on a remote island in the archipelago north of Stockholm, and the low budget and difficulty transporting building materials to the site has influenced the design. The square floor plan has a large central space surrounded by smaller rooms for sleeping, kitchen, bath, and storage in each of the four corners. Between these corner boxes are niches where the top-lit central living area opens in each of the four cardinal directions. Two of the four niches have sliding glass doors recessed toward the living room, creating covered outdoor porches. The house's distinctive peaked form recalls the simple huts built in the archipelago by fishermen and sailors when the islands first began to be populated several hundred years ago.

The exterior is clad in roofing felt. The interior is wood boarding painted pale gray to capture the natural light, while in the porch spaces the boards are left bare to aquire with time a natural gray tone.

2

Söderöra
2005–08

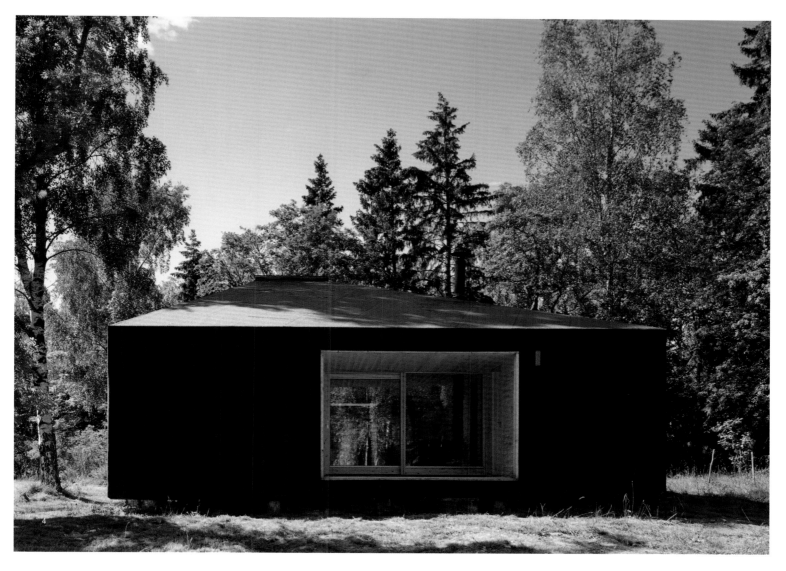

1   *West elevation with covered porch.*
2   *Living area.*

3   *North elevation.*
4   *Southeast elevation with entrance.*
5   *Detail of the southwest elevation. The sea is just visible beyond the birch forest.*

6

6   View from inside looking south over the surrounding landscape.

7   Kitchen and living room.

8   The house is sited between the trees on a pier foundation.

1

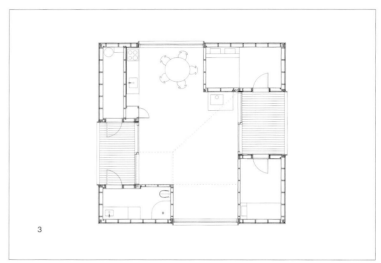

2

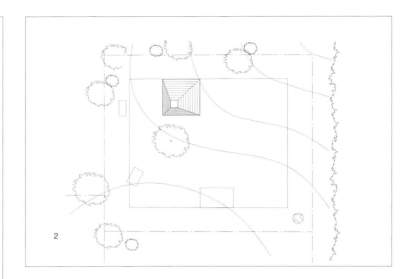

3

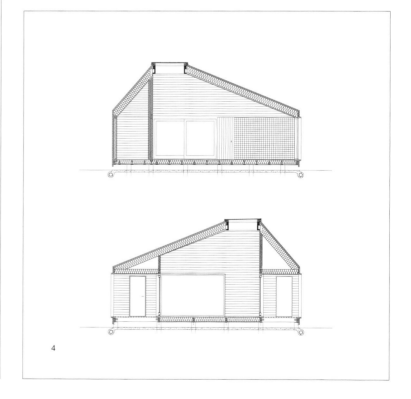

4

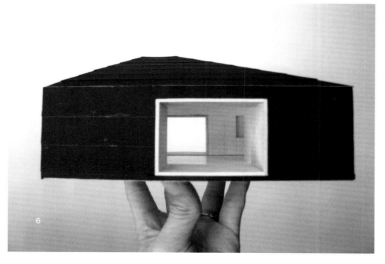

Design team: Anders Rognerud, Bolle Tham, Martin Videgård.

1	*Roof plan and elevations.*
2	*Site plan.*
3	*Plan.*
4	*Sections.*
5	*Aerial view.*
6	*Model.*
7–10	*Construction site photos.*

Moderna Museet Malmö
2008–09

Moderna Museet (the Museum of Modern Art) in Stockholm opened in 1958 and became under the direction of Pontus Hultén one of the world's foremost museums of contemporary art. Moderna Museet Malmö is its newly established branch in the southern Swedish town of Malmö. The city's old electrical power plant, built in the first decade of the twentieth century, had already been transformed into a private museum called the Rooseum in the late 1980s by an art-collecting financier. When he died, the city took over, and in 2006 an agreement was reached to make the building part of the Moderna Museet.

Tham & Videgård were hired to design the new museum after the success of their work on the Kalmar Museum of Art. Nevertheless, the project conditions were quite different. The time schedule from the first preliminary study to the museum's opening was considerably shorter—only eighteen months. The new project also required them to adapt an old building to meet the highest climate and security requirements of an international art museum. The architects resolved the challenge by constructing an entirely new building inside of the old one. It was a strategy that also created opportunities for innovation.

The new addition to the exterior, which holds the entrance, cafe, museum shop, and exhibition space, both contrasts with and plays off of the surrounding buildings. The singular color tone of the stark orange-red facade stands out in its urban context. At the same time, its dimensions are adapted to the adjoining buildings, and even the color resonates with their brick facades.

The box-like form and its perforated surface are also expressive of Tham & Videgård's intention to concentrate their efforts on the large and the small scales, and thereby tone down the building's "intermediate scale." This gives it a more tangible presence both among its immediate surroundings and in the context of the city as a whole. Behind the perforated red panels, the ground floor is fully glazed toward the plaza-like street space outside, which further strengthens the building's relationship to the city.

Inside, the architects have allowed two new staircases to create a kind of loop for visitors to walk between the great turbine hall and the upper gallery above. The stairs are enclosed in walls that accommodate the mechanical systems required in the building program while dividing the turbine hall into three spaces—a large gallery, a children's studio, and a loading area that can also be used for exhibits. The interiors are designed for flexibility—white boxes of varying size, from the more intimate upper gallery to the great turbine hall with its eleven-meter-high ceiling. Tham & Videgårds approach to the existing building has been to use the spaces as far as possible just as they found them, making alterations only as required to create a set of varied environments for art activities. They have preserved the building's industrial character to achieve a tolerant and informal atmosphere.

The entrance space is painted monochrome red, and the cloakroom bright yellow. Together they heighten the contrast between the atmosphere of the galleries and that of the supporting spaces. The brightly colored addition also works as a transition zone between the street and the galleries.

Moderna Museet Malmö
2008-09

1   *Juncture between the preserved entrance portal and the new building.*
2   *Main gallery, the old turbine hall.*

3   *Link between the entrance and galleries, showing the original building's cast-iron columns and beams with segmental brick vaults.*
4   *Children's studio with preserved turbine generator from the former power plant.*
5   *Coat check with yellow lockers. The inside of each door has a quotation from a different artist.*
6   *Elevation facing Gasverksgatan and the museum's entrance plaza.*

7   *One of the two new stairs, this one separating the main gallery from the children's atelier.*
8   *Cafe overlooking the entrance plaza. The facade's perforated sheets recur inside on the ceiling throughout the museum.*
9   *The new gallery.*

10   *The new extension at dusk.*

11   *Facade detail.*

12   *Upper gallery. In the foreground is Robert Rauschenberg's Monogram.*

13   *Cafe looking through the facade and Rauschenberg's logotype from the inside.*

12

13

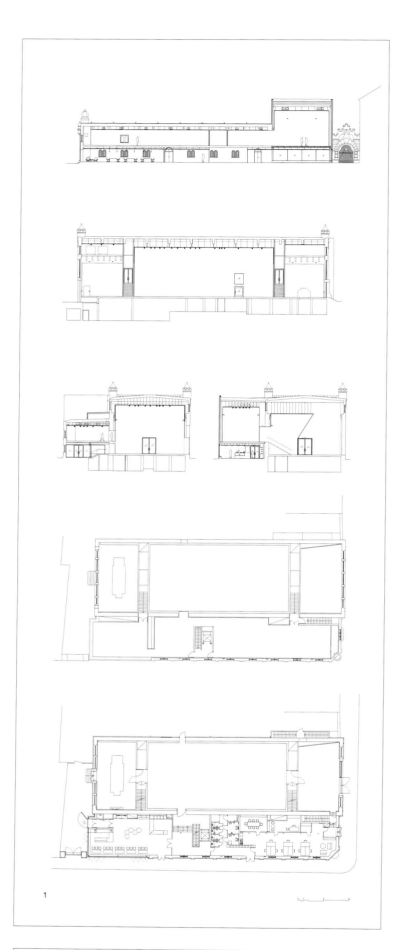

1

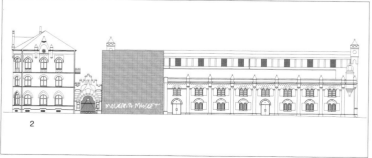

2

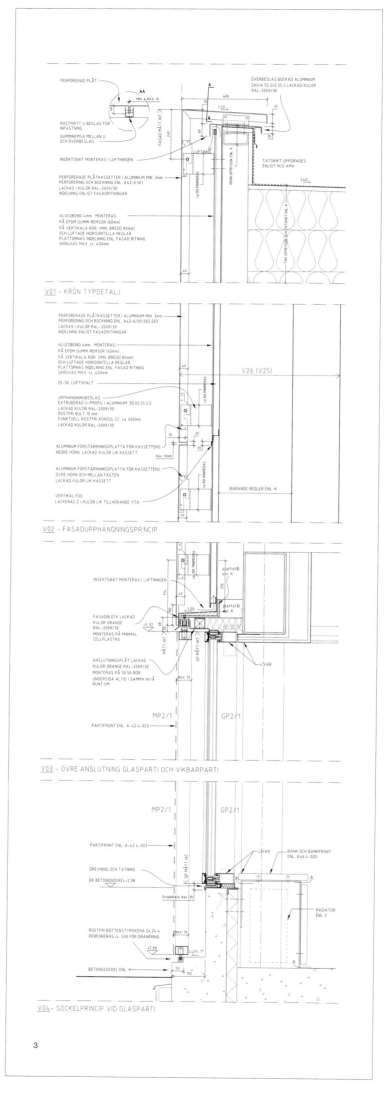

V01 – KRÖN TYPDETALJ

V02 – FASADUPPHÄNGNINGSPRINCIP

V03 – ÖVRE ANSLUTNING GLASPARTI OCH VIKBARPARTI

V04 – SOCKELPRINCIP VID GLASPARTI

3

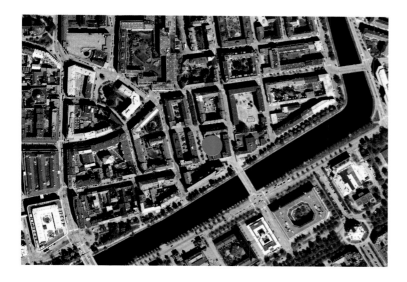

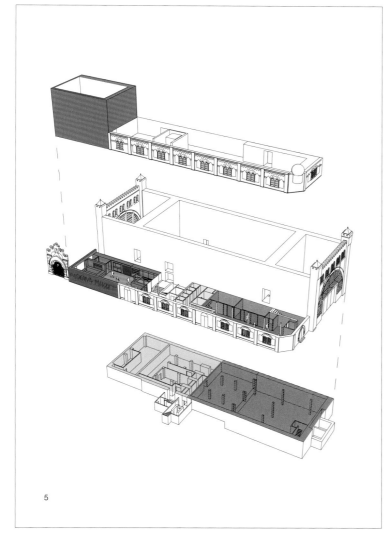

Design team: Mia Nygren, Susanna Bremberg, Helene Amundsen,
Andreas Helgesson, Marcus Andrén, Bolle Tham, Martin Videgård.

1   Building sections and plans.
2   West (front) elevation.
3   Detail section.
4   Aerial view.
5   Building organization diagram.
6   Construction photo showing the new extension before
    facade installation.
7   Test of perforated facade panel with logotype.
8   Installation of new facade.

Garden House
2006–08

The client wanted a garden, and decided to leave an apartment in downtown Stock-holm for a house on the Mälaren lakefront. Tham & Videgård proposed a building that would itself become part of the garden's vegetation by wrapping it in a trellis for vines and seven different plant species—a vertical garden. The project can in fact be defined as a set of three vertical gardens that create outdoor spaces with three different characters. The building—in pragmatic terms, the shelter from the elements—comprises the space between these three garden rooms.

The triangular form of the house is driven by a steep slope that crosses the site on the diagonal. The plan's shape also made it possible to avoid a facade facing due north, which gave better daylighting and better conditions for the vines. A two-story winter garden underscores the home's gradual transition between the interior and exterior, and also helps temper its fresh air supply. A roof terrace offers views across the surrounding landscape.

The entire house is made of wood, and the warm tone of the trellis recurs in the interior paneling. The floor plan is designed around a centrally placed stair. The entry is located in a box that separates the kitchen from the library, two rooms that borrow space from the living room and winter garden. From the open-plan entrance level we move up through a more compact and enclosed second floor, then to an open roof terrace, where we reconnect with the wide-open space of the landscape.

1   *West elevation viewed from the garden.*
2   *South elevation.*

3   *West elevation with patio and garden.*
4   *Detail view of facade trellis. The trellises support seven kinds of climbing plants.*
5   *Acute southwest corner. Inside the corner, behind the trellis, is the double-height glazed winter garden.*

6   *Living room, looking toward the winter garden and patio. The floor finish on the ground level is the polished concrete surface of the slab-on-grade foundation.*
7   *Kitchen with pine plywood paneling.*
8   *Upper hallway with stair leading up to the roof terrace.*

9   *West facade looking into the living room from the patio. With its robust dimensions, the exterior wooden screen is something in between a trellis and a facade.*
10   *The wide lantern gives access to the roof terrace and sky light to the hallway below.*

8

9

10

11

11,13 *Wrapped in wooden trellis, the glazed winter garden is constructed like a greenhouse. The fresh air intake for the house uses air that is preheated by the sun in the winter garden, which saves energy.*

12 *The roof terrace has a view toward Lake Mälaren.*

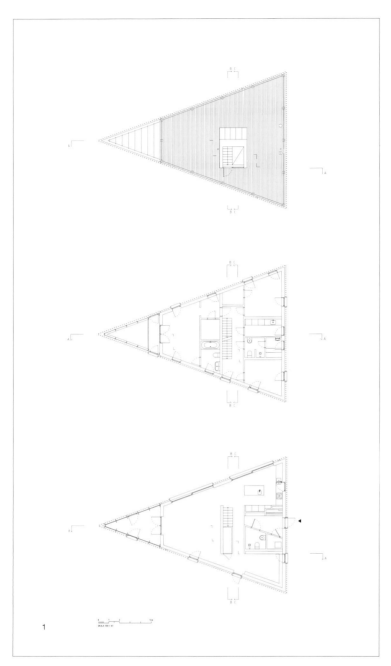

1

3

1   *Plans.*
2   *Facade and sections.*
3   *Site plan.*
4   *Aerial view.*
5–6   *Model, scale 1:25.*
7–8   *Construction site, showing foundation and framing.*
9   *Garage under construction.*

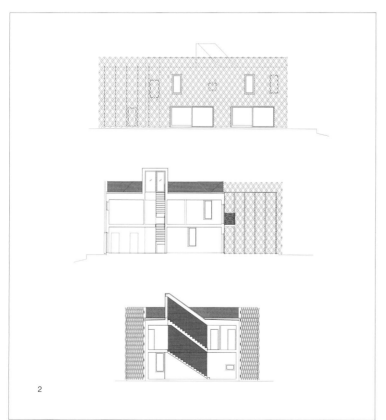

2

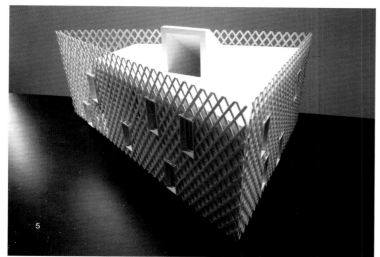

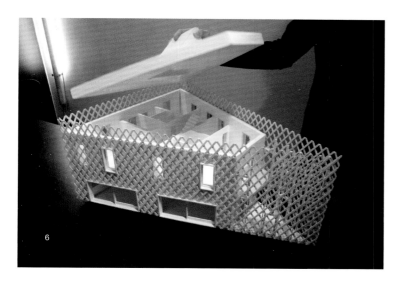

Design team: Fredrik Nilsson, Lukas Thiel, Tove Belfrage, Erik Wåhlström, Bolle Tham, Martin Videgård.

Landscape architects: C-O-M-B-I-N-E / Anders Mårsén, Eveliina Hafvenstein Säteri.

Humlegården Apartment
2006–08

Tham & Videgård's exuberant apartment on Humlegården Park in central Stockholm is designed for a family of four moving back to Sweden after living abroad for some time. The early-twentieth-century building is listed for its cultural historic value, but because of previous heavy-handed renovations, it was impossible to restore the apartment to its original glory. Nevertheless, the architects wanted to relate their design to the home's history, while interpreting that history in new ways. One point of departure was the relationship between the apartment and the park outside, allowing the changing seasons to color the interior. Another aspect of the design is the contrast between the apartment's historic arrangement of rooms in enfilades and the more informal and dynamic spatial order of a modern home. A third aspect is the previous renovations' erasure of most of the finish details that might identify the era of the original apartment.

The autumnal colors of the park have been translated into the tinting of the apartment's hardwood floor and wall paneling. The idea was to use these colors to overlay a new, fluid, contemporary layout on top of the more static nineteenth-century spatial structure. The new ash flooring is custom made, and the different colored pieces are placed individually, arranged with an artful hand. The colors also allude to a tradition of Swedish art and interior design, represented by Josef Frank and Carl Larsson, with a warmer and livelier palette than that of modernism. The colors articulate each room differently, accentuating or dampening the effects of incoming natural light.

In a further comment on the issue of architecture's relationship to time, they have painted every piece of furniture white. The idea was to minimize the effects of age on the individual pieces, thus equalizing their surfaces so they can be perceived and compared on the basis of form alone.

Humlegården Apartment
2006–08

3

1   An enfilade of rooms looking from the living room toward the
    master bedroom.
2   Dining room.

3   Dining room seen from the smaller living room. The entrance foyer
    is visible in the background.
4   Entrance foyer, with the existing leaded-glass balcony doors
    on the right.
5   Small dining room with the kitchen in the background.

6

6   *Master bedroom with windows overlooking Humlegården Park.*

7   *Home office and library. Through the doorway we see an enfilade with the living room, dining room, and kitchen.*

8   *Dining room. At left, the living room's fireplace is visible.*

9   *Kitchen. The dimensions of the herringbone flooring are 180 x 540 mm.*

10   *Library and music room.*

7

9

10

11

11   *Dining room seen from the smaller living room (the children's room).*
12   *Living room with fireplace.*
13   *The children's living room.*

1

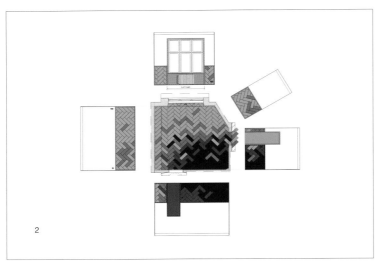

2

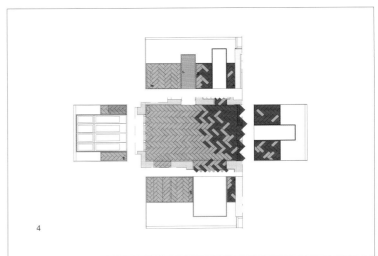

4

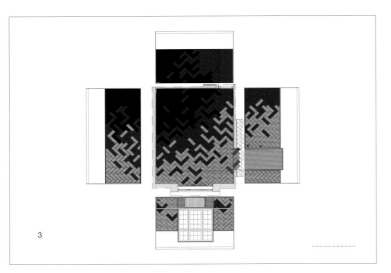

3

1   *Plan.*

2–4   *Foldout plans and elevations for the children's living room, foyer, and master bedroom.*

5   *Aerial view.*

6   *Building facade facing Humlegården. Classified as a cultural historically valuable building, it was built in the National Romantic style in 1912–14.*

7   *Enfilade of rooms during construction.*

8–9   *The new flooring and wainscoting required about seven thousand pieces of hardwood flooring tinted in ten different colors.*

10   *Full-scale test of herringbone flooring on site.*

Design team: Helene Amundsen, Tove Belfrage, Karolina Nyström,
Johan Björkholm, Bolle Tham, Martin Videgård.

Tree Hotel
2008–10

The idea for a Tree Hotel in the little village of Harads in northern Sweden reflects a growing interest in wilderness and ecotourism, for which Scandinavia's large tracts of unspoiled nature offer a wealth of opportunities. Tham & Videgård's task was to design a small hut—a place to spend the night up under the treetops.

Setting aside traditional conceptions of children's tree houses and tree forts, they chose to base their design on the love today's outdoor enthusiasts have for high-tech materials and products (Gore-Tex, Kevlar, carbon fiber, super-light tents, etc.). Their idea was also to find a strategy to let the construction blend in with the sur-roundings, to create a refuge hidden among the trees.

The architects started with a lightweight aluminum-framed cube, four meters on a side, anchored it to the trunk of a tree, and clad it in a skin of mirrored glass. From the outside, the glass reflects the forest all around, minimizing the structure's visual impact in nature. From inside there are wide-open views of the surrounding environ-ment. At night, the glass cube is transformed into a lantern that glows with a warm light. To prevent birds from striking the glass, the surface was to be laminated with a film that reflects ultraviolet light.

The little hotel room is dimensioned for two guests. The plywood-clad interior holds a sitting room with a queen-sized bed, a kitchenette, and a bathroom. There is even a roof terrace accessed from inside. The hut is reached by a rope ladder or from a rope bridge connected to the neighboring trees.

The Tree Hotel is operated in conjunction with an adjacent inn that can provide meals and other services. Six huts, each designed by different architects, have been built in the first phase of construction.

3

5

1 *At dusk, behind the mirrored glass the window openings are visible, with their views over the surrounding landscape.*

2 *The hotel cabin, with its system of hanging bridges and wire stays. The structure is tied to the tree trunk with clamps that don't harm the tree.*

3 *Cabin interior clad in pine plywood. The pendant light was designed by T&V in connection with this project.*

4 *Evening picture. The illuminated interior is visible through the square window openings.*

5 *The reflective cladding of the exterior even covers the bottom of the cabin.*

6 *Interior with skylight.*

7 *Facade at dusk.*

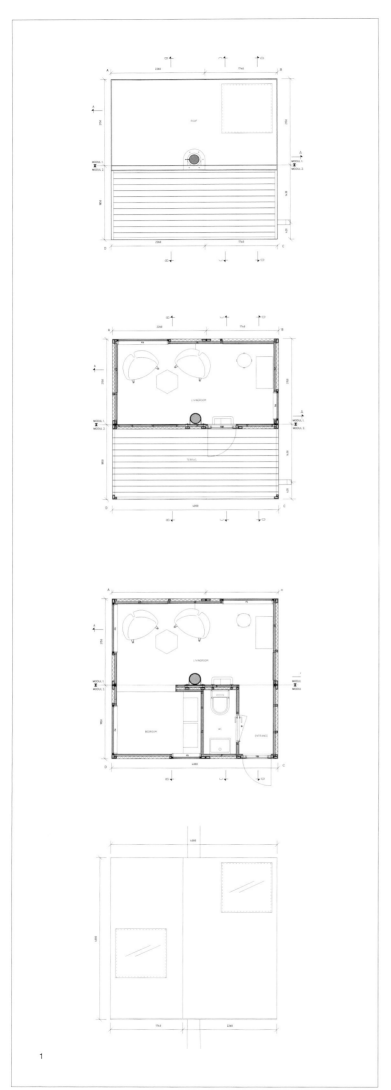

1

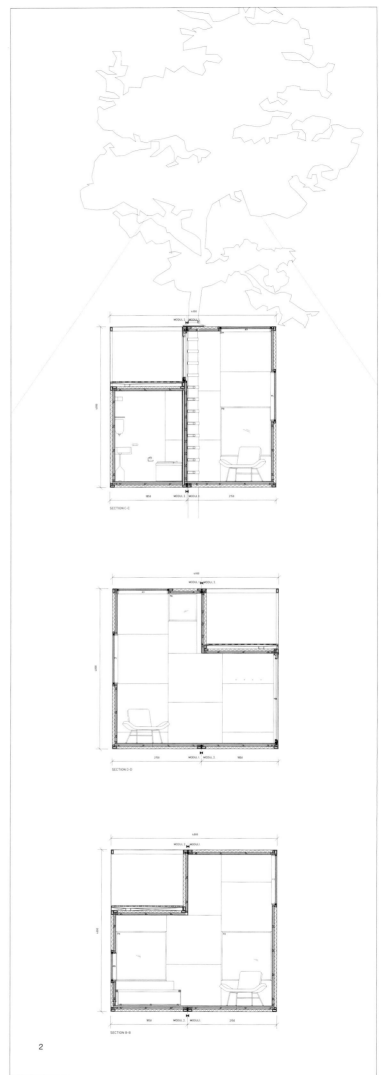

2

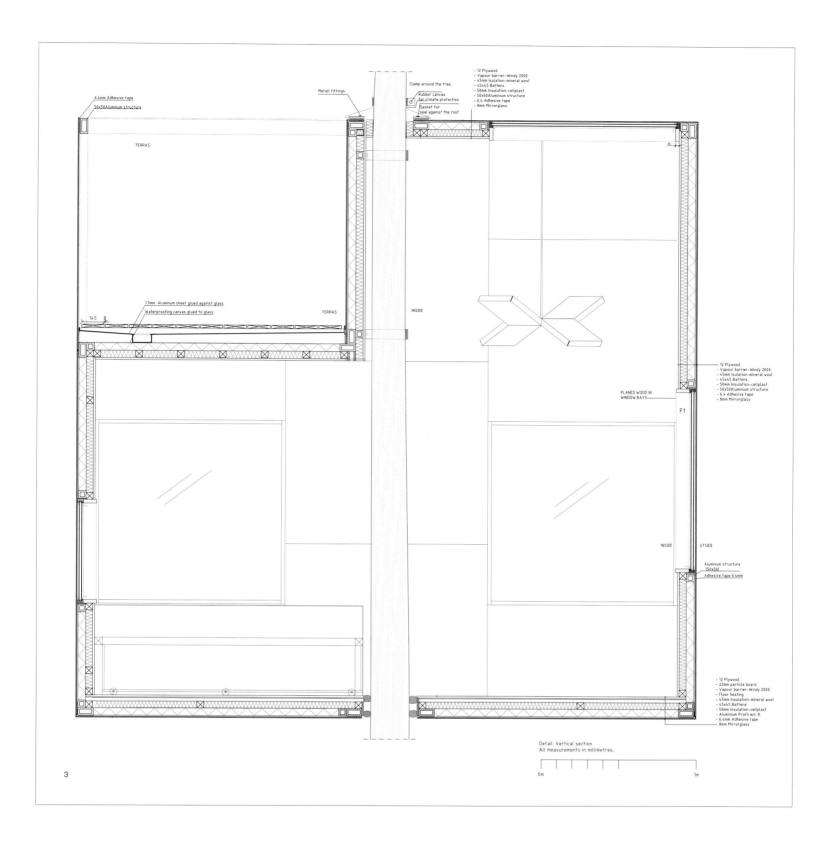

6.4mm Adhesive tape
50x50Aluminum structure

Metall fittings

Clamp around the tree.

Rubber canvas
for climate protection

Gasket for
seal against the roof

- 12 Plywood
- Vapour barrier-Windy 2000.
- 45mm Isulation-mineral wool
- 45x45 Battens
- 50mm Insulation-cellplast
- 50x50Aluminium structure
- 6,4 Adhesive tape
- 8mm Mirrorglass

TERRAS

TERRAS

INSIDE

1.5mm Aluminum sheet glued against glass
Waterproofing canvas glued to glass

145   8.

- 12 Plywood
- Vapour barrier-Windy 2000.
- 45mm Isulation-mineral wool
- 45x45 Battens
- 50mm Insulation-cellplast
- 50x50Aluminium structure
- 6,4 Adhesive tape
- 8mm Mirrorglass

PLANED WOOD IN
WINDOW BAYS

F1

INSIDE

UTSIDE

Aluminum structure
(50x50)
Adhesive tape 6.4mm

- 12 Plywood
- 22mm particle board
- Vapour barrier-Windy 2000.
- Floor heating
- 45mm Insulation-mineral wool
- 45x45 Battens
- 50mm Insulation-cellplast
- Aluminium Profil enl. K.
- 6,4mm Adhesive tape
- 8mm Mirrorglass

Detail. Vertical section.
All measurements in millimetres.

0m   1m

3

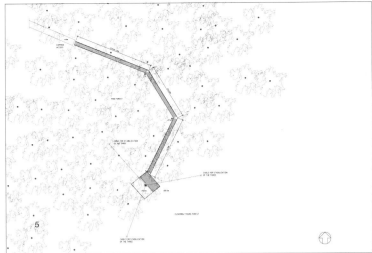

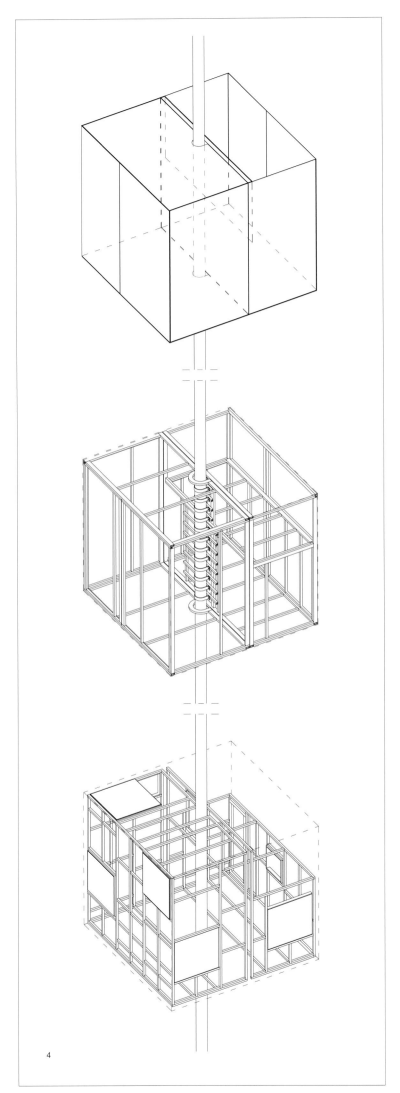

1   *Plans and elevation.*
2   *Building sections.*
3   *Construction details.*

4   *Axonometric schematic showing the component layers of the structure. The cube was built in two halves that were lifted into place and joined together around the tree trunk.*
5   *Site plan.*
6   *Aerial view.*
7–8   *Presentation images of the proposed interior.*
9   *Frame being transported on the roads of Norrland.*
10–11 *Construction photos.*

Design team: Andreas Helgesson, Julia Gudiel Urbano, Mia Nygren, Bolle Tham, Martin Videgård.

Works

1   *North elevation.*
2   *Facade detail. The facade is vertical spruce siding with an oil-based stain. The robust window surrounds are of 50 mm thick pine.*
3   *View from the south.*
4   *Plans, section, elevation.*

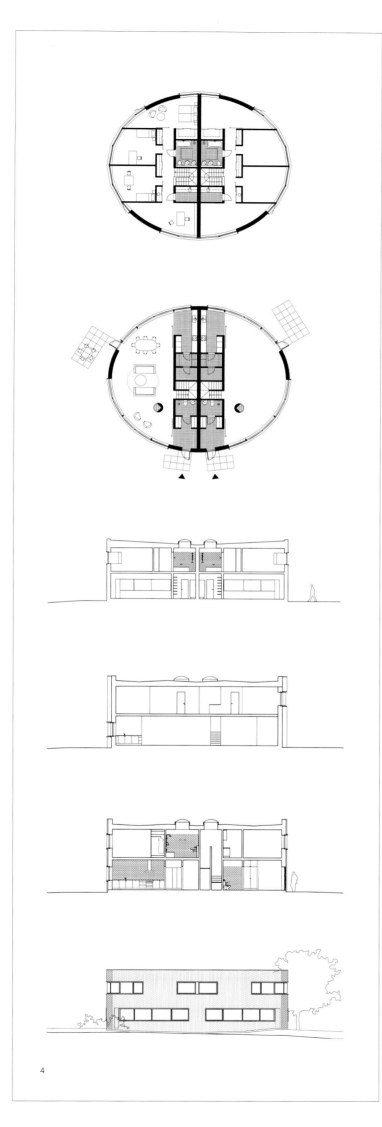

Double Houses
2005–06

The site is caught between two residential neighborhoods of differing character: to the east, a typical development of single-family homes; to the west, a newly constructed five-story apartment building. Tham & Videgård's two new pairs of duplex homes are freely placed on their relatively small lot. Their cylindrical forms preserve the continuity of the outdoor space, avoiding divisions into front and backyards.

At ground level is an open living area for socializing. Ribbon windows in an arcing facade give the space 180 degrees of view. The architects have described it as a giant bay window that heightens the presence of daylight and vegetation inside the home.

The floor plan is straightforward. The two homes are adjoined along a thick wall where kitchens and baths and mechanical systems are concentrated. This scheme means that the small rooms have at least two or three right-angle corners, which makes them easier to furnish. All storage is located along a top-lit corridor outside the bedrooms.

The buildings are constructed of concrete cast into insulated concrete forms. The thermal mass of the concrete and its double insulation save energy by minimizing the temperature swing inside. The floors are heated with radiant water tubing cast into the slab that is connected to a heat exchanger. The facades are black-painted vertical wood siding. The walls and ceilings are painted white and the floors are oiled, white-pigmented hardwood.

Design team: Tove Belfrage, Lukas Thiel, Josefine Wikholm, Bolle Tham, Martin Videgård.

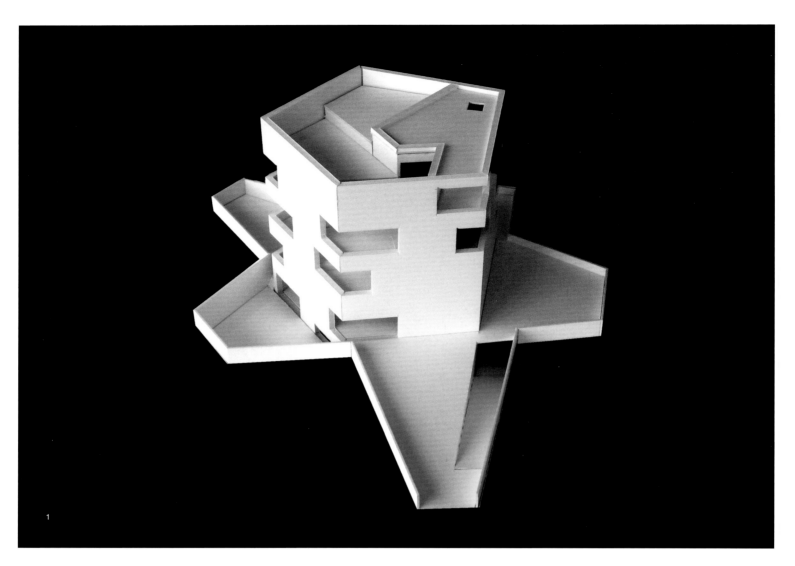

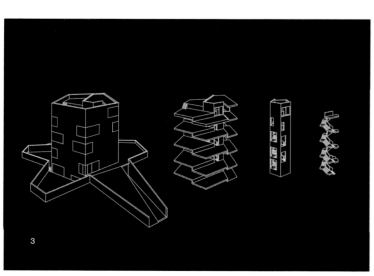

1   Working model, scale 1:50.
2   Interior study, showing the juncture between the plywood-clad interior partitions and the concrete stairwell core.
3   Illustration, showing exterior, floor levels, stairwell, and stair.
4   Massing study, showing garden with birches.
5   Plans.

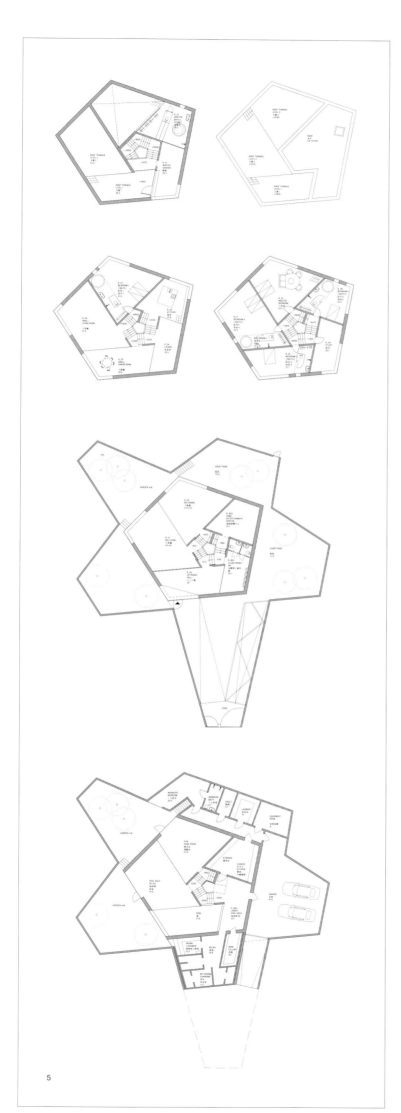

Ordos 100
2008–

The Ordos 100 development is an initiative of a water company and municipality in the Ordos Desert of Inner Mongolia, China. Herzog & de Meuron, who designed the "Bird's Nest" Olympic Stadium in Beijing, were asked to select one hundred prominent young architecture firms from around the world to design each one a 1,000 m² villa. The master plan for the development was designed by the multitalented Chinese artist Ai Weiwei.

Tham & Videgård's villa is about creating a vertical topography that enriches and complements the horizontal Ordos plateau. The design is based on an ascending spiral of spaces that begins with a swimming pool on the lowest level and ends with a roof terrace that opens to the sky. A stairway winds around the structural core of the house, surrounded by rooms at ever-increasing elevations. The spaces required by the program brief are thus spread across a climbing series of interior terraces that are visually interconnected and yet clearly articulated as individual spaces. The result is an informal arrangement in which representational, social, and private rooms are all linked in a continuous flow of space.

The building's footprint, an asymmetrical pentagon, reflects the architects' idea of remaining neutral toward the directional axes on the site. It is a response to the unusual challenge of creating architecture in such an indeterminate situation: this essentially uninhabited desert plateau is to be populated with a hundred villas in the span of only a couple of years.

The plan makes use of only part of the lot for yard space around the villa; the rest is allowed to blend into the development's common park grounds. Four courtyards are appended to different faces of the building, each enclosed by a low wall and planted with grass and birch trees to create a contrast to the surrounding arid, sandy landscape. The building is to be made of exposed concrete (facades, floors, roof, and stairwell), plywood panels, etched glass, and ceramic tile for the pool. All the windows are fixed and flush-mounted with stainless steel hardware.

Design team: Carmen Izquierdo, Fredrik Nilsson, Eric Engström, Tove Belfrage, Johan Björkholm, Julia Schönbrunn, Bolle Tham, Martin Videgård.

5

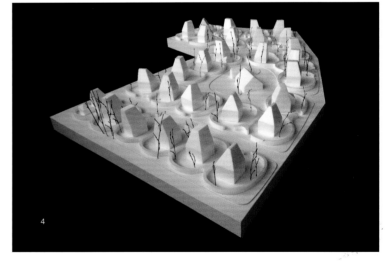

1   Illustration of the village at night.
2   Aerial view of the proposed development.
3   Aerial view.
4   Model photo.
5   Sections and plans (house types A and B); elevations and sections.
6   Site plan.

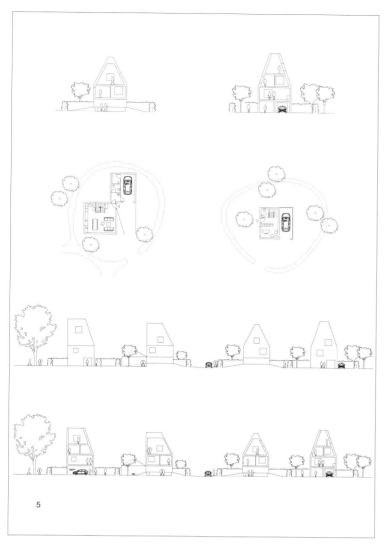

5

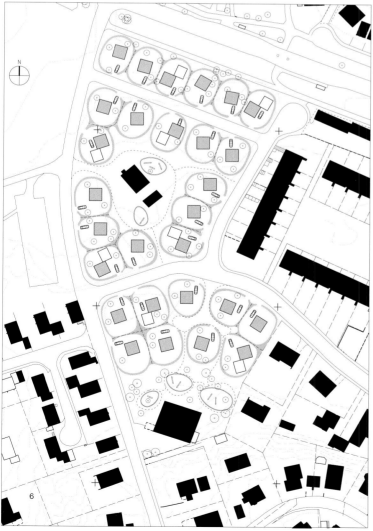

6

Vertical Village
2009

This project arose in response to Stockholm's growth and the consequent demand for new developments of single-family homes. The site is a property already incorporated into a neighborhood of such homes near Lake Mälaren. Tham & Videgård designed a kind of "garden cottages" that connect with the existing housing types but also add a new character to the neighborhood. Each house is placed in the middle of a rounded parcel that is surrounded by a tall hedge. The curving hedges give a soft edge to the area's streets and to the fluid public places and pathways between the homes. The lots are the same small size (200–300 m²) as those of the typical row houses nearby, but by building up, the architects have freed up valuable yard space. The result is a more compact version of the traditional suburban housing development.

The architects have described how the basic concept was born from the history of gardening, plant nurseries, and greenhouses that is commonly associated with the area. Also important was the character of a nearby landscape of Stone Age graves and burial mounds. Still another source of inspiration was a small community of allotment gardens in Nærum, Denmark, designed by C. Th. Sørensen in the late 1940s; but Tham & Videgård's plan alters the spatial properties of that community by raising its low hedges to become like walls and working with larger houses placed in the center of their round lots.

The firm has described these tall houses as a new typology that arranges the rooms of a traditional home more vertically. The development has two house types. The A model has three floors, with the living room and kitchen at ground level and an extra smaller building to be used as a garage or winter garden. The B model has four floors, with garage/studio/or winter garden at grade and common areas one level up. The upper floors of both the three- and four-story homes look out over the park-like structured landscape, giving each an experience of both enclosed and wide-open outdoor space.

Two existing buildings are to be integrated into the new development: a former country store will be converted to a daycare center, and an old community center will continue to operate in a new context.

Design team: Helene Amundsen, Marcus Andrén, Bolle Tham, Martin Videgård.

1   Southeast elevation.
2   Southeast facade with shutters open. The wood siding is more robust
     than is typically used today and thus connects to a building tradition
     that gives the house a more rustic character and a more durable
     facade. It is painted with a mixture of traditional Falu red distemper
     and tar oil (known locally as "red tar"), which adds to the facade's
     durability. Prominent surrounds give the standard windows a distinctive
     character.
3   Upper level living room.
4   Site plan.
5   Plans and section.
6   Axonometric illustration showing the building's mass, frame,
     light wells, and fenestration.

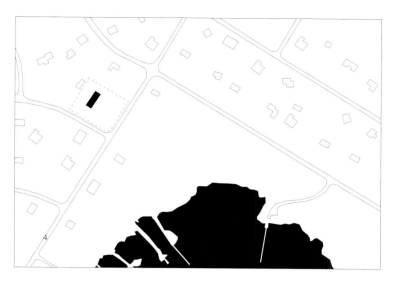

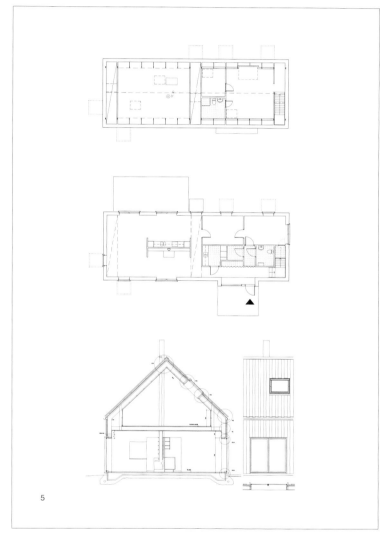

Karlsson House
2000–02

The clients for this private home were a couple in their sixties who wanted a new house with space for visiting children
and friends. The site in Tidö-Lindö, near the town of Västerås,
had beautiful views of the large Lake Mälaren. Throughout the
area, the original stock of smaller vacation houses had gradually been renovated or replaced, mostly by standardized pre-
fabricated homes.

The budget was limited, and to minimize the construction
cost the architects chose to base their design on the Swedish
barn—a simple utilitarian building, and a type that was at home
in the surrounding cultural landscape. The entire structure was
planned on a 1.2-meter module using standard components
wherever possible, which made the resulting cost substantially
lower than for a typical single-family home of the same size.

The facades as well as the roof are clad with wood siding painted with traditional Falu red distemper, emphasizing the prismatic form of the building volume. The wooden roofing recalls
historical Swedish building traditions. The windows are complemented by grill-like shutters—"brise-soleil" that both reduce
the amount of solar heat gain and liven up the facades.

The house was planned in two parts: a fully furnished home on
the ground floor and an unfinished second floor that could be
furnished in the future when the need arose. The upper level
also includes three light wells that create variations in both
the volume of space below and the daylighting conditions of
the home. The plan is laid out to give the owners a variety of
choices as they move about the house. The windows are freely
distributed over the facades and roof to vary the experience of
moving through the interior, and to make the most of the views
of Lake Mälaren and the surrounding vegetation.

*Design team: John Billberg, Claes Sörstedt, Fredrik Olsson, Bolle Tham,
Martin Videgård.*

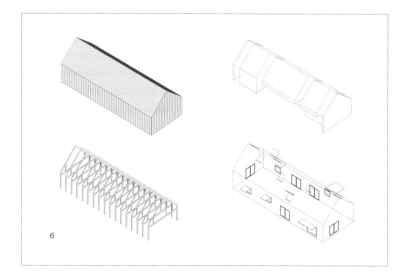

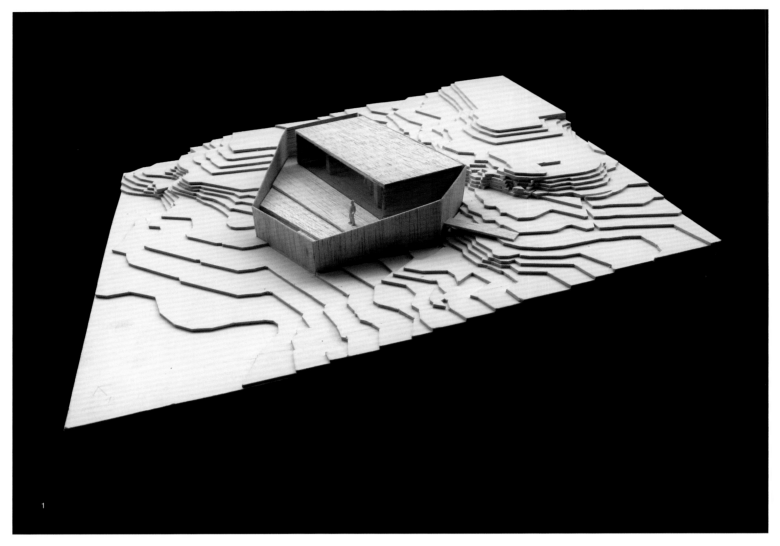

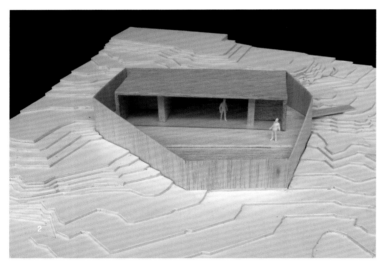

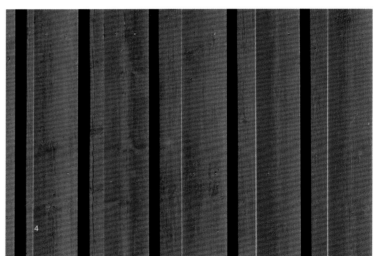

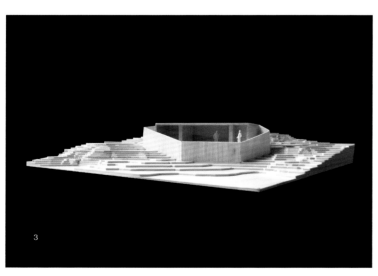

1–3   Model, showing west elevation facing the water.
4   Facade reference, Falu red distemper on sawn wood.
5   Site plan.
6   Entrance level plan.
7   West and south elevations.
8   Illustration of the view from the living room.

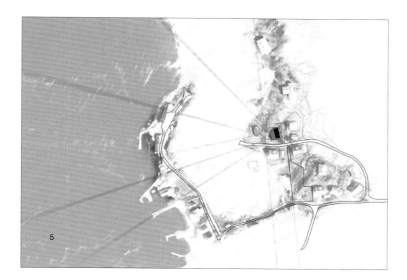

5

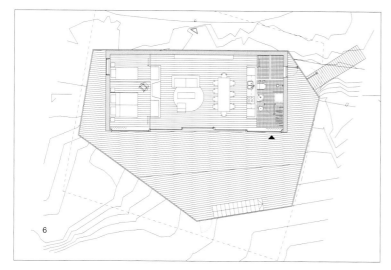

6

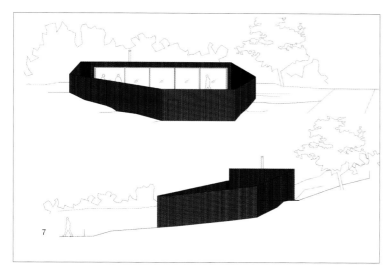

7

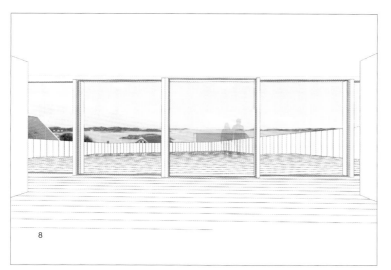

8

Circuit House
2010–

The fishing and seafaring community of Fiskebäckskil, in the archipelago on Sweden's west coast, goes back to the Middle Ages. Since the nineteenth century it has been a beloved seaside haven for summer residents. The clients for the Circuit House are a couple who work in the fields of art and archeology. They wanted a small house with a patio located and designed to take advantage of the view of the sea to the west while providing protection from the wind and visual privacy from the nearby neighbors of this relatively sense community.

Tham & Videgård wanted to create a sheltered place for the house by surrounding it with a plank fence that follows the terrain in the shape of an irregular pentagon. The corners of the fence are located at breaking points where the slope of the site changes and the fence is the same height all around, its top edge always parallel to the ground. It thus reflects the topography in a nearly prismatic form.

As the fence drops away with the descending terrain, the patio space opens up to the view and the afternoon sun; at the back of the house, the fence rises to provide enclosure to the north and east. Outside, the irregular pentagon creates a variety of differently shaped garden spaces that transition in part to areas of exposed bedrock.

The house itself is a simple box placed at the top of the site. The construction and detailing of the house are intended to be as simple as possible: concrete pile foundation, wood frame, sliding glass doors. All of the surfaces are either rough-sawn or planed pine. All wood is painted in traditional Falu red distemper on the outside, and whitewashed on the inside. The roof is to be vegetated with sedum.

Design team: Mia Nygren, Jamie Hay, Marina Huguet Blasi, Bolle Tham, Martin Videgård.

1   *South elevation with the boardwalk that passes along the building.*
2   *Illustration at dusk, showing the building's characteristic silhouette.*
3   *The visitor center in winter.*
4   *Auditorium.*
5   *Exhibition space and reading area.*
6   *Cafe overlooking the surrounding natural landscape.*
7   *Site plan.*
8   *Plan, elevation, section.*

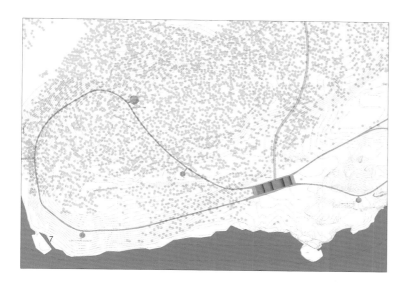

Naturum Laponia
2009

The point of departure for this project—submission for an invited competition—was an opportunity to establish a new place for recreation and learning in the globally unique natural environment of Stora Sjöfallet (the Great Lake Falls region). It is one of only two places in the world classified as world heritage areas for both culture and nature. The objective was to create an attractive and surprising outpost to celebrate that heritage and to educate the public about it. At the same time, the architects wanted to design a building that is functionally adapted to the sensitive natural site while making it accessible in a respectful way.

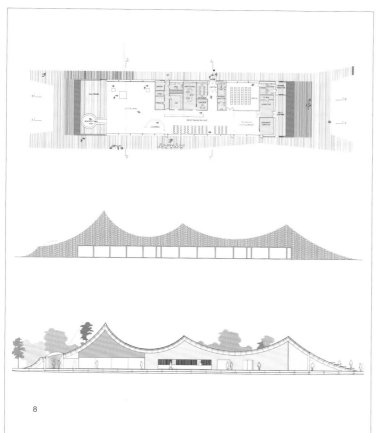

Tham & Videgård's basic idea was a design in which both the building and its associated boardwalks rest lightly on the ground like a kind of loosely laid wooden duckboards. Their model was the Laplanders' nomadic structures, which are abandoned or buried when they wear out so that all of the materials used biodegrade and are returned to the earth. The visitor center rises from the boardwalk, an all-wood structure with a roof like a tent—or like a silhouette of the mountains.

The building is located at the juncture between the entrance road and two boardwalks that wander through the landscape. The site is adjacent to a place where the Laplanders still gather together their reindeer before the grazing period, and the design makes space to accommodate that activity. The building's distinctive roof profile rises from the landscape; beneath it, long glass walls provide a wealth of daylight and views. On the entrance side, the glazing is wrapped in the same wood ribs used in the boardwalks and roof. These ribs part to mark the entrance, with its airlock entry, cloakroom, and toilets. From the entrance, the building opens up with views of the surrounding landscape. Inspired by the way the great spaces in that landscape are formed, as mountains and forests alternately converge and open up, the architects have satisfied the programmatic requirements for the various rooms and departments with a plan that provides a separate space for each in a context that remains open and contiguous. A series of draping roofs, like inverted transverse barrel vaults, articulates a sequence of alternately high- and low-ceilinged spaces. The floor plan is designed to give visitors an immediate understanding of the center's layout, allowing them to orient themselves at once among its different parts.

Design team: Carmen Izquierdo Làzaro, Johan Björkholm, Mårten Nettelbladt, Andreas Helgesson, Marcus Andrén, Dennis Suppers, Bolle Tham, Martin Videgård.

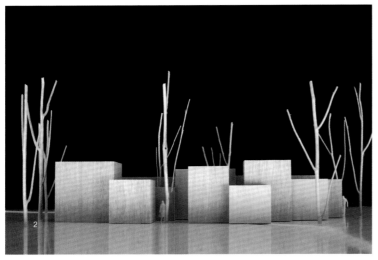

1–3   *Massing studies with wood model, scale 1:100.*
4   *The building is to be constructed of reclaimed brick.*
5   *Plan.*
6   *Elevation and sections from the south.*

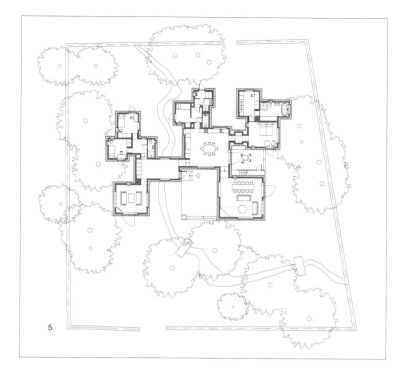

5

Brick House
2008–

This Brick House was designed for exactly the same lot as the Botanic Garden House. This time the home is spread out over a single story, but like its predecessor it is carefully adapted to the natural features of the site. If the earlier design was a light, transparent pavilion, this one consists of a series of solid, loosely arranged volumes constructed from reclaimed handmade bricks. Tham & Videgård have linked together these brick blocks to create both interior and exterior spaces and spatial connections, giving the lot—despite its limited size—an abundance of different small places. The intention has been to make the lot feel larger by creating a complex of spaces that cannot be overviewed from a single point. The building and its site are interwoven so that each makes visible qualities in the other. One of the site's main features, a small creek, even passes through the house, bridged over by the entrance hall.

Design team: Konrad Krupinski, Lukas Thiel, Eric Engström,
Mårten Nettelbladt, Bolle Tham, Martin Videgård.

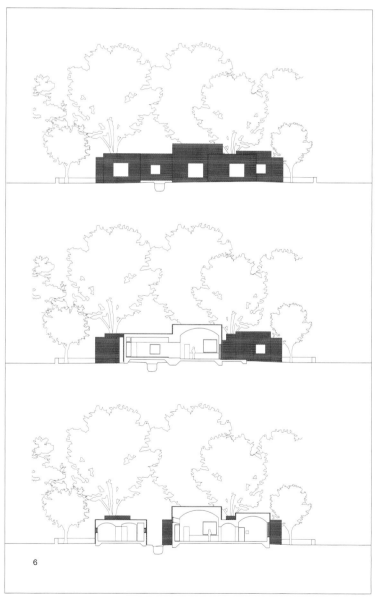

6

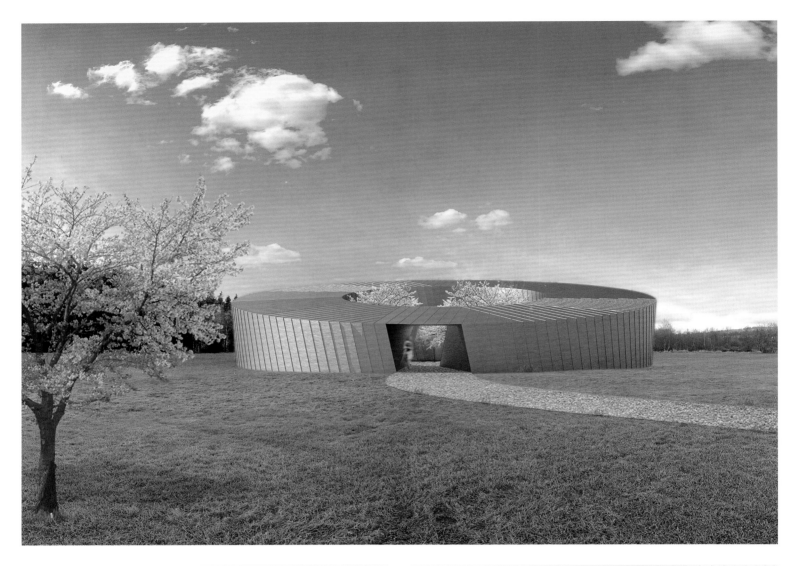

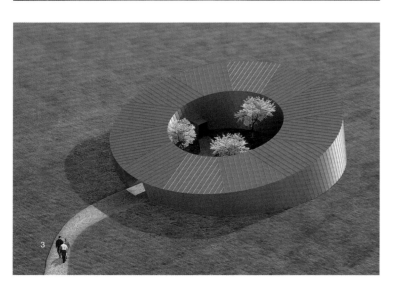

1 West elevation.
2 Courtyard with passage and entrance.
3 View of building form from above.
4 Titanium facade sample.
5 Aerial view.
6 Building sections and plan.
7 Construction details for window niche.

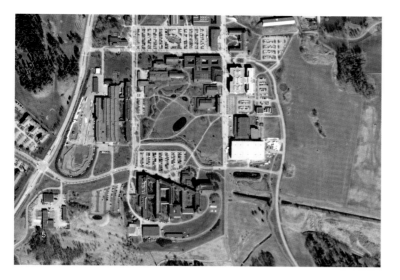

Electron Microscope
2010–

The project to design a building for a new electron microscope began with an initiative from Linköping University and Akademiska Hus, a campus property developer and management company. The microscope is one of the most sophisticated in Europe and is intended to facilitate new materials research and new international research exchanges.

Because of the microscope's sensitivity, it was important to select a site with as few disturbances as possible and to achieve the highest technological quality of construction. After exploring solutions in which the facility would be built underground in the vicinity of existing research buildings, it was determined that a better strategy would be an above-ground building in a more remote location with optimal conditions for a stabile foundation.

Tham & Videgård's design is inspired by and reflective of the high-tech research being conducted at Linköping University. The building's form is a sloped cylindrical ring with a round inner courtyard. Its standing-seam titanium cladding helps shield it from outside magnetic fields. The walls of the cylinder are canted at right angles to the slope of the roof in a way that recalls the firm's early restaurant pavilion for Stureplan in Stockholm. The idea is for the building to lie like a scaleless, abstract, shimmering object in the landscape. Its precise geometry, metallic surface, and apparently temporary placement give it a high-tech and yet dreamlike appearance.

Design team: Andreas Helgesson, Mårten Nettelbladt, Anna Jacobson, Andy Penuela, Bolle Tham, Martin Videgård.

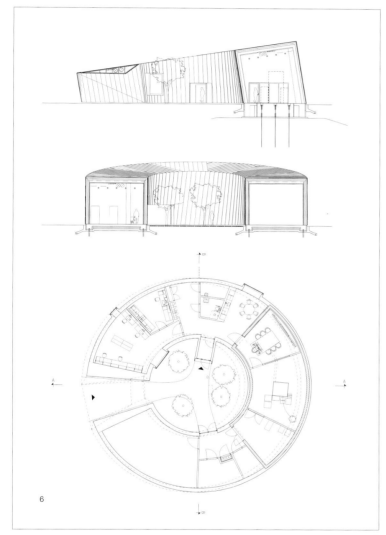

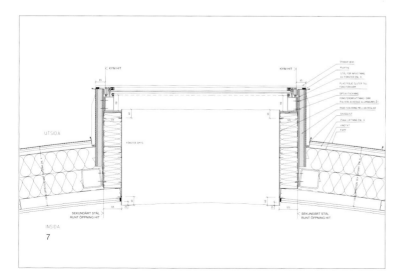

1   *View of the house from the east.*
2   *Southwest elevation at dusk.*
3   *Entrance, with its projecting roof of cast-in-place concrete.*
4   *View from dining room looking toward living room.*
5   *Site plan.*
6   *Elevations, plans, sections.*

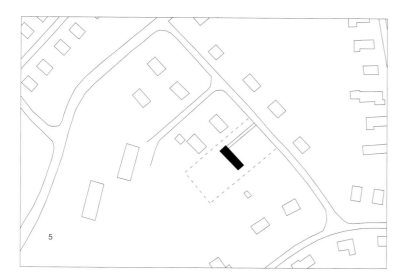

5

House K
2004–05

House K in Stocksund, outside of Stockholm, is one of Tham & Videgård's long and narrow single-family homes. The area is well represented in early twentieth-century Swedish architecture, with nearby homes including Lars Israel Wahlman's Tallom House (1906) och Erik Gunnar Asplund's Snellman House (1918). Many of the other houses in the area are from the same period and Tham & Videgård have taken up both the earthy shingle-style character of National Romantic architecture and the slender elegance of the 1920s style of Swedish Classicism. Their building makes use of the full breadth of the site, clearly separating the front yard from the garden at the back. The architects have likened the house to a wall between the two outdoor spaces within which they have made a place to live.

On the interior, Tham & Videgård have established an interplay between the two levels that gives variety to the sequence of spaces in terms of volume and ceiling height. They have also created diagonal lines of sight through the house that enhance the sense of spaciousness. Otherwise the floor plan is quite clear. The ground level is an open plan apart from a box containing the entry, guest toilet, and stair; at the top of the stair a corridor leads to several second-floor bedrooms.

The building's frame is cast-in-place concrete, which is visible in a perforated entrance roof that is just seven centimeters thick. Using insulated concrete forms helped keep the construction cost low. The facade is clad in black-stained plywood panels, a modern way to achieve the earthiness of the surrounding National Romantic style homes. The interior is white with floors and millwork of ash.

Design team: Henric Lundén, Bolle Tham, Martin Videgård.

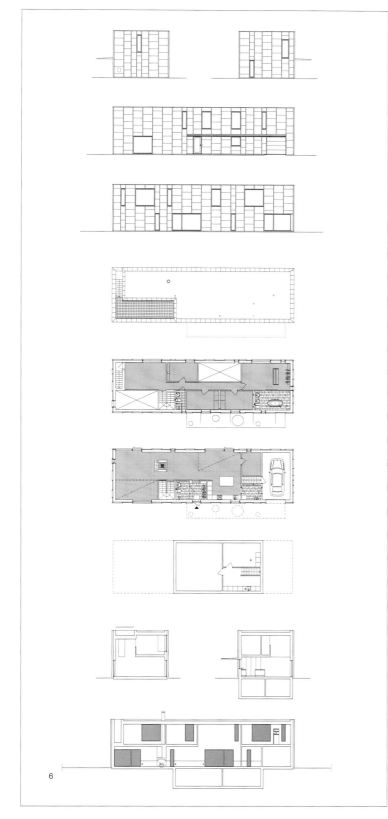

6

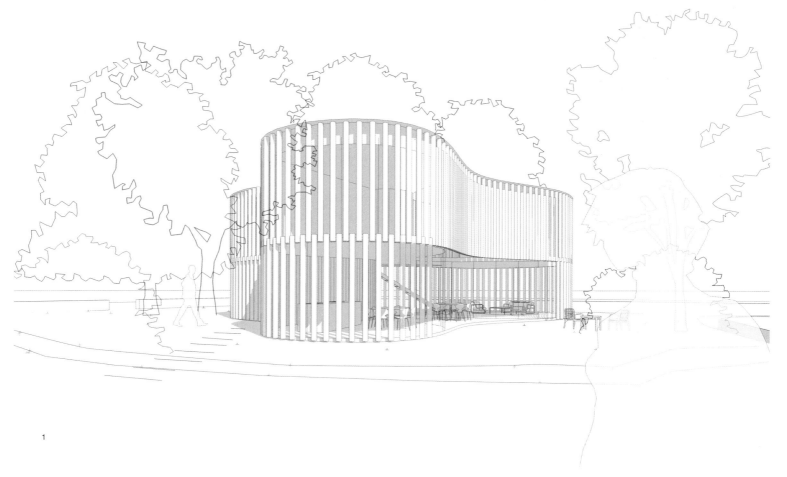

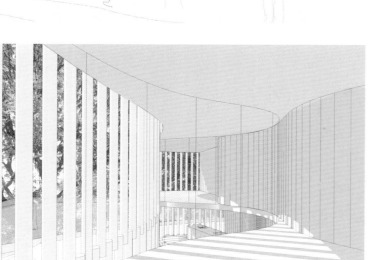

1   *Illustration of house viewed from the southwest.*
2   *View from the southeast.*
3   *Illustration of second-floor interior.*
4   *View from interior onto patio, garden, and sea.*
5   *Elevation, showing the house nestled among the trees.*
6   *Plans.*
7   *Site plan.*

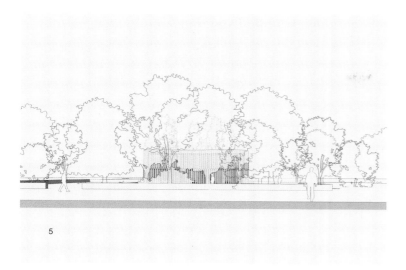

5

Botanic Garden House
2006

For Tham & Videgård, the design of the Botanic Garden House was one step in the process that would lead to the Brick House. The site is a gradually sloping lot overlooking the Kattegatt, the waters separating Sweden's west coast from Denmark. It is planted with several different species of trees and bushes with a variety that suggests a botanic garden. A luxuriant canopy of leaves creates a kind of green ceiling over most of the lot, and a small creek wanders through it, contributing to the idyllic character of the place.

Since the trees and bushes provide shelter from the periodically heavy winds, the architects decided to carefully inscribe the house between the tree trunks, and to develop its plan as a fluid, organic space. The intention was to make the house a part of the garden—thus its rounded form. Its curvilinear facade has two layers: an outer screen of thick vertical poles and an inner climate barrier entirely of glass. The layers diverge in places to create an outdoor room on the ground level and one upstairs.

The spacing between the poles gives the facade the character of vertical blinds. With the aid of a hydraulic system, portions of the upper and lower pole screens can be raised and lowered, overlapping them to create regions of greater enclosure and others of complete exposure. In this way, the relationship between inside and out can be varied and calibrated to the current weather and how the spaces are being used.

Design team: Erik Wåhlström, Tove Belfrage, Bolle Tham, Martin Videgård.

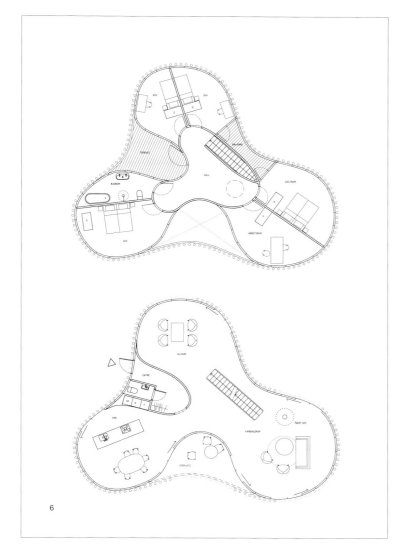

6

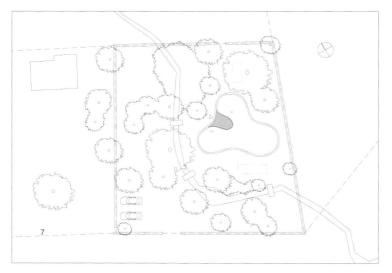

7

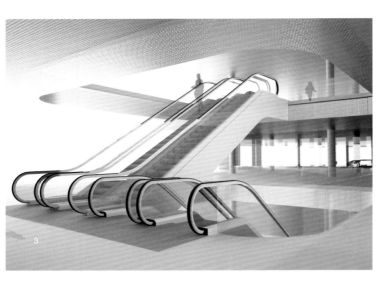

1   View of building from the south.
2   Interior view, showing escalators and the semitransparent
    silk-screened glass facade.
3   Interior view.
4   Elevation facing Stora torget with the main entrance.
5   Site plan.
6   Detail section of facade.

Åhléns Department Store
2009–

The new Åhléns Building in Uppsala is a department store building with both shops and offices. Half of the building incorporates an existing concrete slab-column frame, while the other half is an entirely new structure on a vacant adjacent lot.

Tham & Videgård have based their design on Uppsala's urban character and scale, and created a distinctive building with a clear identity. The objective has been to produce a building with great functional longevity, a building concept malleable enough for its design to survive intact while accommodating a variety of different programmatic and zoning demands and adapting to the varied urban spaces on different sides of the building.

The organic plan form has several different points of entry, creating new paths through the block, but it still unites the building's different businesses under the single shared identity of its distinctive and coherent shell. The idea of the facade's curving contours is to lead the eye around its corners, establishing spatial continuity from one side of the building to the next. The glass panels vary in reflectivity and transparency, giving the building a fluctuating appearance as you move around it. The softly undulating facade elements also create overhangs that articulate the locations of entrances and shops.

Tham & Videgård address the typology of a department store —typically a large, windowless box—by varying the form and attributes of their glass enclosure to create a dynamic visual impression. With such distinctive facades, the building also serves as an orientational landmark in the surrounding neighborhood.

The facade panels are conceived as extraclear (low-iron) glass silk-screened with a reflective raster, a solution that allows a gradual transition between transparent and mirrored portions. The reflective facade also serves as a rain screen and contributes to the building's energy efficiency.

Design team: Andreas Helgesson, Mårten Nettelbladt, Alina Scheutzow, Jamie Hay, Chris Paxton, Harriet Brisley, Julia Gudiel Urbano, Bolle Tham, Martin Videgård.

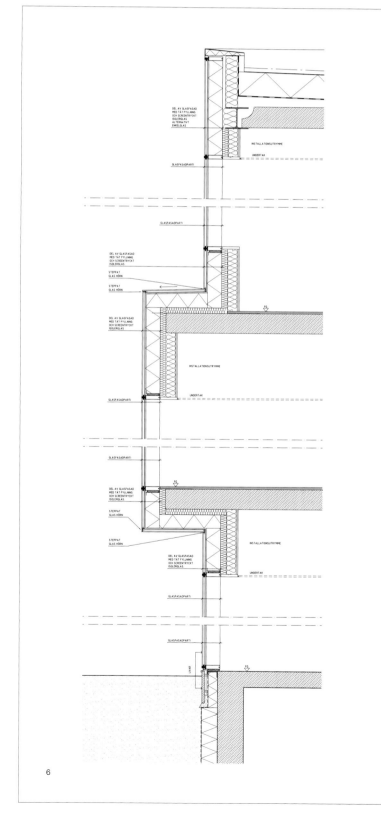

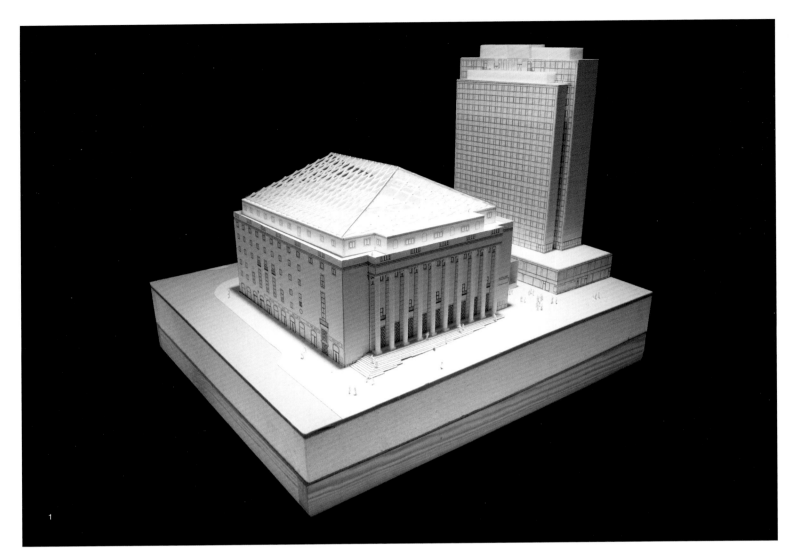

1 Working model showing the roof structure, scale 1:100.
2 Illustration of the new rooftop theater, bar, and restaurant.
3 Illustration, showing the new restaurant looking out over the city to the south.
4 Entrance elevation toward Hötorget at dusk.
5 Ilustration showing vertical circulation.
6–7 Building sections.

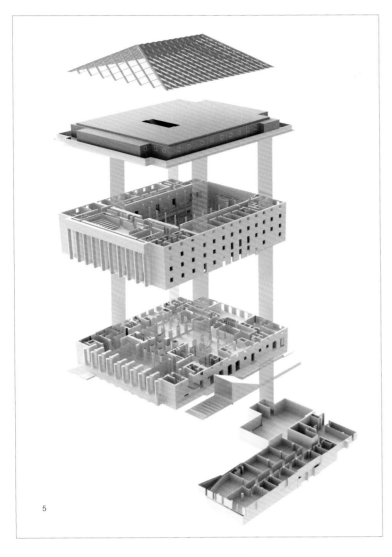

5

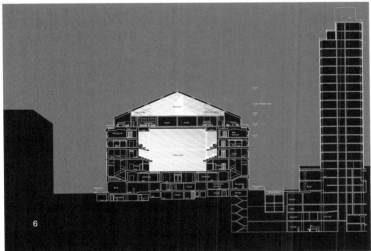

6

7

Stockholm Concert Hall
2009–

Ivar Tengbom's Stockholm Concert Hall is one of the most important public buildings of the period of 1920s Swedish Classicism, and it is located on a site that is dense and charged in terms of both history and urban planning. Completed in 1926, the building now needs to be renovated and expanded to meet the functional demands of a modern concert venue. The new spaces that are needed include an additional performance stage, a restaurant, exhibition spaces, and rehearsal and orchestra spaces. In a parallel commission of several firms, Tham & Videgård were the only ones to propose an addition built on the roof of the existing building, which needs to be reinforced anyway for acoustical reasons. Their scheme was judged to be the strategy most likely to be able to preserve the building's existing qualities while satisfying the new demands, and they were commissioned to continue working on the project.

Tham & Videgård's proposal was based on several thoughts and ideas. One decisive choice was the determination to develop the concert hall's character as a freestanding building. Their analysis of the building's place in its urban context indicated that each of its four facades plays an important role in the streetscape, while its top does not exert such presence. This suggested that it would be wise to avoid an addition that connects the concert hall to neighboring buildings and street spaces.

Tengbom himself had described the ceiling of the concert hall in terms of a kind of heavenly light—an idea that could now be fully realized by providing public space under a glass roof open to the sky. The new stage and restaurant would also enjoy magnificent views over the city. Building on the roof made efficient use of the existing building's circulation as well, although it still needed to be modified and expanded.

The sensitive urban environment and historically charged building, together with the program's demanding technical and spatial requirements, make this one of the firm's most complex and delicate projects to date.

Design team: Mia Nygren, Andreas Helgesson, Anna Jacobson, Mårten Nettelbladt, Carmen Izquierdo, Julia Gudiel Urbano, Suzanne Prest, Harriet Brisley, Chris Paxton, Bolle Tham, Martin Videgård.

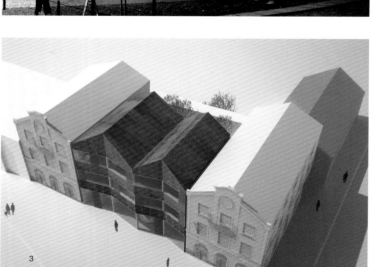

1   Elevation overlooking the harbor and the Baltic Sea.
2   Building at night.
3   Massing study of the block.
4   Material sample of corten steel.
5   Aerial view.
6   Plans, sections, elevations.

Simrishamn Apartments
2010–

The site for this infill project in Simrishamn lies in the old part of this medieval city, down in the harbor area and close to Stortorget, the main square. On either side of the lot were buildings with both apartments and retail space. The area between them was separated from the street by a wall and partially occupied by rudimentary single-story storage and garage buildings. The brief called for redeveloping the entire lot to create a new whole that would integrate all of the existing functions.

Tham & Videgård's proposal creates two floors of apartments with space for retail at ground level. Each apartment is designed around a large living area with windows overlooking the harbor. The new facade is folded slightly in and out, articulating spatial divisions in the open-plan living space within, and creating bay windows with views down the street in both directions. At the back, smaller rooms and protected balconies surround a courtyard with a west-facing patio.

The double gable roof over the new central portion embraces the scale and gabled form of the existing buildings, while a facade of rust-red Corten steel gives the new part a character all of its own. The robust material is durable in the exposed coastal climate and also establishes a connection to the activity of the harbor.

Design team: Mia Nygren, Christine Lavelid, Bolle Tham, Martin Videgård.

6

1   *Illustration of the central courtyard space.*

2   *South elevation.*

3   *Working model of terraces.*

4   *Diagram showing the building's limited footprint and the four branches that form terraced space between them. At bottom are height comparisons with several well-known buildings: in relative terms, the building's dimensions are small.*

5–6   *Sections.*

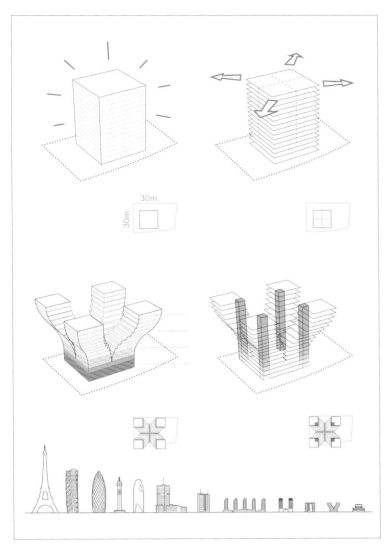

Vällingby Parkstad
2010

The proposal for a new mixed-use tower at the entrance to Vällingby Parkstad (Vällingby Park City) was developed for an invited competition. Råcksta, a former office park for the Vattenfall electric company outside of the Stockholm suburb of Vällingby, was to be transformed into a complete residential neighborhood. To clearly signal the district's new character, the brief called for a tall entrance building that would serve as a landmark. Tham & Videgård's design is a twelve-story apartment building that branches out at the fourth level into four identical building arms. The lower floors have retail and office space, while the branches above hold apartments with terraces.

The architects describe the design as a "new typology" and call the building a "tree building"—a name that plays off both the idea of a park city and the unusual form of the building. The tree-like structure frees up the grounds around the building while making good use of the air space above for apartments and terraces. The idea is to create apartments with high-rise views and the more intimate outdoor spaces of a row house. In this the building may be seen as a vertical interpretation of the row houses already found in the surrounding neighborhood.

Each floor of the upper branches of the building can be planned for one, two, or three apartments. Beneath them, on levels 4 and 5, the base of the building could be divided into up to thirty-two compact student apartments.

Besides the tree reference, the architects have also described the space between the four upper branches as "an inverted variation of the unique outdoor space formed beneath the Eiffel Tower in Paris." That reference should also be noted for the significance the famous tower has had in defining and promoting the city's identity.

The building's form is bold, but the architects have also held fast to the garden city ideal and refrained from proposing a truly large-scale tower. In comparison with other tower buildings, its twelve stories seem rather modest. The building's structure and technology are designed for economic and energy efficiency.

Design team: Eric Engström, Mårten Nettelbladt, Mia Nygren, Jamie Hay, Andy Penuela, Marina Huguet Blasi, Bolle Tham, Martin Videgård.

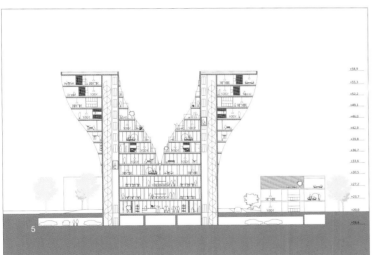

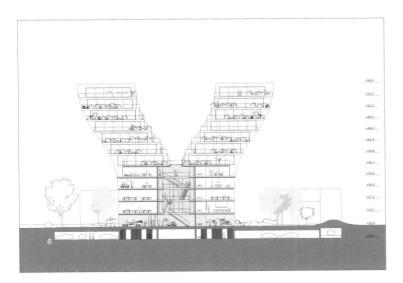

1   *West elevation. Blue-black stucco with fixed solid oak windows.*
        The solid panels are doors and ventilation openings.
2   *Stairwell with a continuous staircase to the roof terrace.*
3   *Living room. The floor is finished with asphalt tiles.*
4   *View from the south.*
5   *Sections, facade, and plans.*

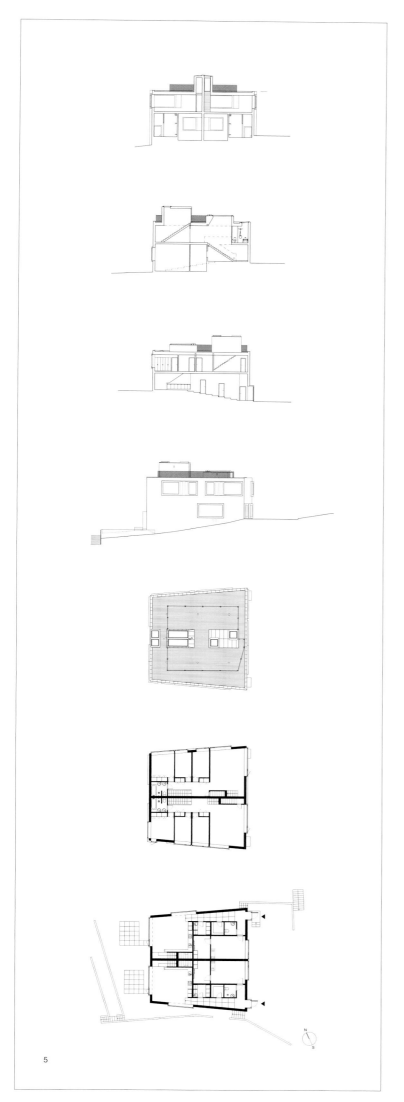

Double House
2004–05

Tham & Videgård's duplex house in Danderyd, outside Stockholm, is unusual in the history of Swedish architecture both as a type and in its design. The two back-to-back homes are organized around four large spaces on different levels (including a roof terrace) that are connected in a spiral. The two homes are mirror images, apart from some variations to accommodate differences in their surroundings and their orientation to the sun.

The architects' intension was to make the four principal spaces as general and therefore as flexible as possible. At the same time, they vary from one to the next in terms of volume, daylight, and views. The roof terrace forms the largest social space for both homes.

The duplex house makes use of the maximum allowable floor area and building height. It is framed in cast-in-place concrete, and the facades have been stuccoed in a dark blue-gray tone. The projecting oak window frames articulate the building volume and create deep window niches inside.

Design team: Henric Lundén, Elin Andreassen, Bolle Tham, Martin Videgård.

5

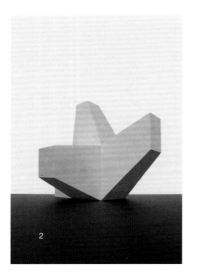
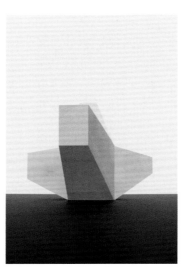

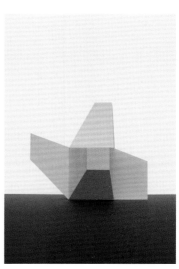

1   *Illustration showing interior projections.*
2   *Model studies.*
3   *Illustration of Cloud Chamber in the gallery.*
4   *Plan of gallery, section through gallery, plan of Cloud Chamber.*

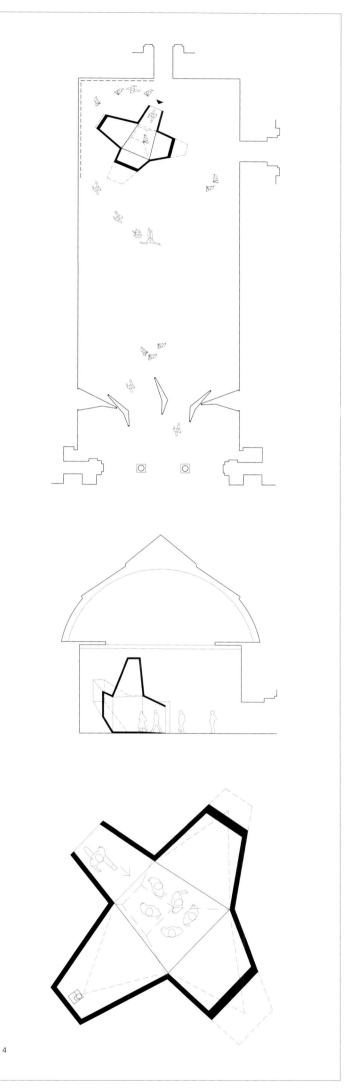

Cloud Chamber
2009–10

Tham & Videgård designed Cloud Chamber for the Victoria & Albert Museum's exhibition "1:1—Architects Build Small Spaces." Nineteen different architects from various parts of the world were invited to use the museum as a "test site" to "examine notions of refuge and retreat." The firms were given different themes on which to base their designs. Tham & Videgård were to explore the duality Performance/Fiction (other dualities included Cocoon/Womb, Playtime/Dreamspace, and Laboratory/Shed).

The architects wanted to create a pavilion in which a simple and modest structure offers an experience of boundless space. Cloud Chamber comprises a small room surrounded by back-projection screens, with four appendages that house projectors, all of it framed in wood. Inside, visitors are completely immersed in time-lapse video of swirling clouds; the exterior is conceived as a stylized wooden cloud, or a fallen star. A notable contrast is established between a tangible exterior and an intangible, indefinable interior. Sound and possibly wafts of fresh air would further enhance the sense of being someplace entirely removed from the museum.

The office also proposed that when the exhibition was over, the pavilion could be used as a play space or relocated to a nearby park. The projectors would be removed and the steeply sloping surfaces stepped to make a kind of play sculpture. The piece's robust wooden construction was designed to withstand such use.

Design team: Carmen Izquierdo, Julia Gudiel Urbano, Harriet Brisley, Bolle Tham, Martin Videgård.

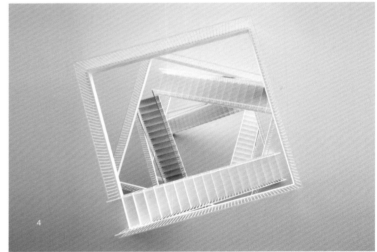

1   *View of buildings from the southwest.*
4   *South elevation overlooking the water.*
2   *Working model (facade study).*
3   *The square-shaped rotating stairwell.*
5   *Site plan.*
6   *Plans and sections.*

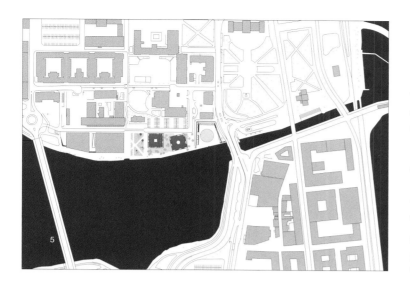

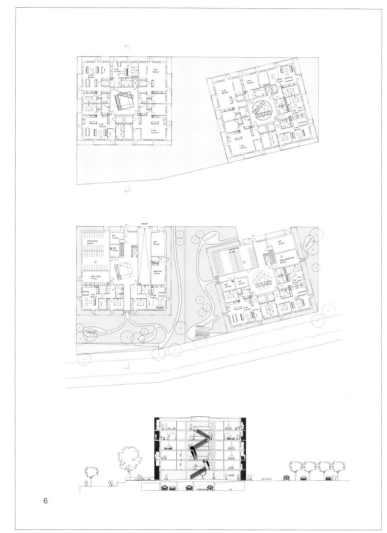

Västra Kajen
2009–

Tham & Videgård won first place in an invited competition to design a pair of apartment buildings on Västra Kajen (the Western Quay) in Jönköping. For a strip of property along an inlet of Lake Vättern, the brief's program statement actually called for a number of slab buildings, a scheme intended to provide as many of the apartments as possible with views of the water. After analyzing the urban scale of the site, Tham & Videgård were the only firm to disregard the suggested slab solution. They decided that the situation called for larger building volumes, and proposed two nearly cubic apartment blocks. The buildings were rotated in relation to each other, one aligning with the street at the back of the site and the other with the embankment. This created a more dynamic relationship to the surrounding buildings and also strengthened the orientation toward the water.

The architects took advantage of the large building volumes to work with the vertical circulation at the core of each. The buildings' depth allowed them to give each a central courtyard, a kind of social forecourt or atrium in which crisscrossing flights of stairs create a varied ascent. One of these courtyards is square in plan, the other round.

Despite the compact building volumes, the architects were able to give every apartment a balcony with a water view. These balconies are staggered so that each has two stories of space to the next one above. At the outermost plane of the buildings, they are wrapped in a ribbed veil that strengthens the impression of the buildings as two solid blocks, while filtering the light passing into—and out from—their interiors.

Openings in the outer facade layer correspond to the double-height balconies, and these large cutouts make the buildings appear from a distance to have fewer than their six stories. The architects have said they wanted to give the facades a kind of colossal order. The monumental openings are intended to negotiate the transition between the smaller residential scale of the buildings and the grand scale of the city and waterway that surround them.

Just as the two courtyards were given different forms, the buildings' facades are colored differently to give each its own identity.

Design team: Eric Engström, Carmen Izquierdo, Anna Jacobson, Harriet Brisley, Helene Amundsen, Mårten Nettelbladt, Andreas Helgesson, Julia Gudiel Urbano, Karolina Nyström, Bolle Tham, Martin Videgård.

1 *West elevation with main entrance and entrance plaza.*
2 *View of courtyard from the southeast.*
3 *Cafe with access to terrace and cinema.*
4 *Cinema foyer.*
5 *View through reception toward the sea.*
6 *Exploded axonometric diagram.*
7 *Longitudinal and transverse sections.*
8 *Model, scale 1:200.*

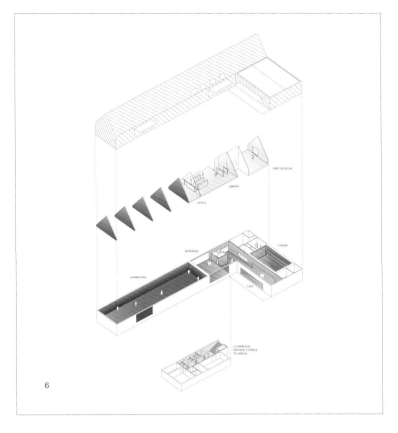

6

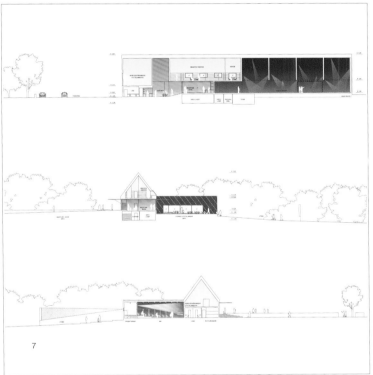

7

Bergman Center
2010–

Tham & Videgård were awarded the commission to design the Bergman Center after winning an invited competition. The center's mission is to manage and develop the legacy of Swedish film and stage director Ingmar Bergman, who began living and working in the vicinity of the competition site on the island of Fårö in the 1960s. The brief called for converting and expanding an old school into a visitor center with a cinema, exhibition space, cafe, library, and a museum of local culture. Besides preserving the existing school buildings, Tham & Videgård were intent on embracing the local cultural landscape in their design.

The architects' scheme joined the two existing buildings together under a new steeply pitched gable roof. They were able to accommodate the program with little change to the old school buildings: essentially only non-load-bearing interior partitions were removed. The new center's black exterior sets off its vivid red interior. The color derives from traditional cinema decor, though the tone in the cafe and reception is somewhat lighter. The exhibition hall, on the other hand, is as black as a camera obscura.

The exterior takes the form of a large barn-like volume clad in black roofing felt. The architects wanted to take up the local building tradition, with steeply pitched gable roofs, but also introduce something new and unexpected. Spatially, they worked with the tension between the entrance courtyard in front of the building and the park space that faces the sea at the back.

Design team: Carmen Izquierdo, Andy Penuela, Mia Nygren, Mårten Nettelbladt, Bolle Tham, Martin Videgård.

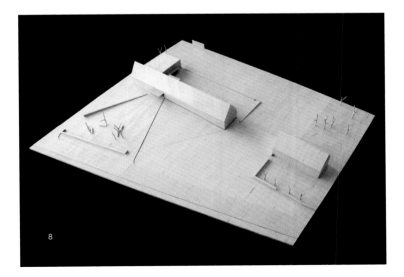

8

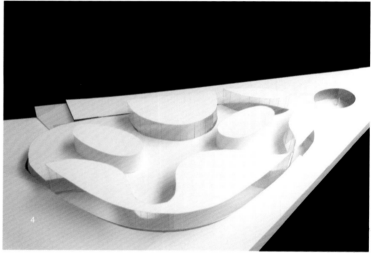

1   *South facade with entrance.*
2   *Illustration of design studios.*
3   *Illustration of atelier space.*
4   *Ground floor model study.*
5   *Plans. Level 6, faculty and researcher offices; levels 3–5, design studios; level 2, mezzanine offices; level 1, ground floor of the architecture school, and the new entrance building for the university campus.*

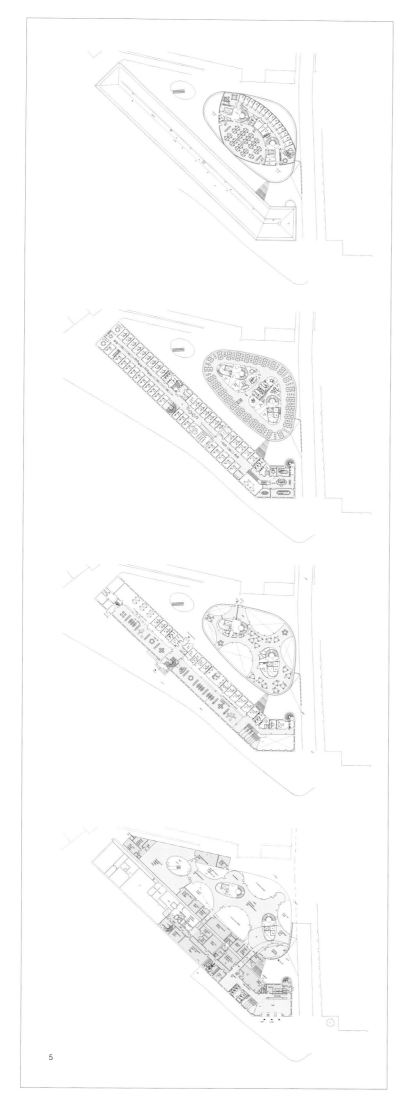

School of Architecture KTH
2007–

The project for a new School of Architecture building at the Royal Institute of Technology (KTH), where Bolle Tham and Martin Videgård themselves were students, is the result of an invited competition held in 2007. Besides the new architecture school, the competition brief also included a new entrance building and plaza (called the KTH Campus Entré). Tham & Videgård was the only firm who chose to clearly distinguish the two functions in separate buildings.

The architecture school is designed as a compact, rounded volume floating within an existing triangular courtyard, a definitively freestanding building. Its Corten steel facades relate to the red brick buildings that surround it. The architects have chosen to emphasize the building's individuality as well as the flow around and through it. That flow is generated by the places they create both outside and inside the building, and is based on their analysis of how a university campus works. As in Kalmar, the goal has been to fit the new building into its context without eliminating existing pathways.

Shared functions such as art studios, exhibition spaces, and workshops are consolidated at the entrance and mezzanine levels. Design studios and faculty offices are on the next three floors, followed by a top level for administrative offices and a roof terrace. Central to the layout is the idea of making the entire school—every floor of it—available to all, whether they be students, teachers, researchers, or visitors.

The interiors are designed to be robust and flexible. Curving walls create a free flow of contiguous space and enhance the sense of openness rather than enclosure.

Design team: Carmen Izquierdo, Mia Nygren, Andreas Helgesson, Anna Jacobson, Mårten Nettelbladt, Benjamin Mandre, Susanna Bremberg, Lukas Thiel, Fredrik Nilsson, Anna-Lisa Pollock, Marina Rotolo, Bolle Tham, Martin Videgård.

Architecture and the Reality of Learning
An Ongoing Project

Johan Linton: In the summer of 2007 you won a widely publicized parallel commission to design a new building for the School of Architecture at KTH (the Royal Institute of Technology in Stockholm). At the time you were still closer to your own education than Gunnar Henriksson, Klas Anshelm, and Helge Zimdal had been when they designed the architecture schools in Stockholm, Lund, and Gothenburg about forty years ago. It was also a different time: one of the four commissioned proposals came from an internationally acclaimed office in Japan—SANAA—something that could not have happened when the older schools were built. Swedish architects don't often get a chance to express themselves on the subject of architectural education through the design of a new building, and it would be interesting to hear a little about your thoughts and assumptions in the project. For example, how does your design relate to other schools of architecture? What qualities and shortcomings from earlier buildings have you incorporated into your work?

Bolle Tham and Martin Videgård: The architecture schools where we studied were KTH, Belleville in Paris, Konstfack (the University College of Arts, Crafts, and Design in Stockholm), the KKH (Royal University College of Fine Arts) School of Architecture, and (Alvaro Siza's) school in Porto (Portugal). During our student years, the building one studies in serves as a kind of full-scale model, an example to be evaluated and from which we can learn to read a building. One consequence is that the school itself has the potential to be an educational tool, a world to explore. Experience shows that renovations of existing buildings often turn out to be the most appreciated schools, and this has been demonstrated by studies (compare with how artists vote for the best museums or places to exhibit their work). They give the school an informal quality, and thus offer a kind of open and neutral platform on which to build. That sort of straightforward architecture is inspiring and something we are sympathetic to, since it also provides leeway for continuous and gradual development: the architecture school as an open platform on which various educational strategies and organizational models can take turns over time. For example, Belleville (before its renovation), the new Konstfack, and Gunnar Henriksson's building (in Stockholm) can be read as attempts in that direction, while Siza's Porto school has a definitive and extremely fixed spatial structure.

JL: How have you approached the issue of spatial organization?

BT & MV: The site on the KTH campus, with its very tangible cultural and historical context and its physical limitations, could be described as the opposite of a blank slate situation. The new school is inserted into an existing courtyard space with existing pathways and is located adjacent to the university's main entrance, with Erik Lallerstedt's original brick buildings from the early twentieth century. By contrast, Lund's architecture school, the University of Stockholm, and the Porto school were starting from scratch, built on essentially undeveloped sites.

One point of departure for us was to study possible circulation patterns on the campus and through the courtyard with the goal of siting the building without reducing the number of pathways. This led us to the idea of including and encouraging circulation all around and through the building as a way of thoroughly integrating and anchoring the new school with the site. Then we thought that the building's entire section—not just the ground level—could be made accessible to everyone, whether teachers, students, researchers, or visitors. This openness is reinforced in plan by the continuous, rounded forms of the floor plan, in which different program spaces or functions can adjoin one another almost without walls. Views and paths are extended through a structure with spatial conditions more akin to a landscape than a traditional institutional building. In terms of program, the building is divided vertically, with shared functions (art studios, workshops, exhibit spaces) on the entrance level, intermediate levels for design studios and project spaces, and shared meeting rooms and roof terraces on top.

JL: What qualities did you see as important to achieve in your work with the project?

BT & MV: The dimensional conditions of the triangular courtyard site gave us a thick building that posed challenges but also provided some opportunities. One challenge was to create enough space and light throughout each floor plate, even deep into the core of the building. One opportunity was to exploit the advantages of a consolidated plan in which all of the functions required in the building program can be located directly adjacent or in close proximity to one another, which creates efficient internal connections. Another opportunity offered by the thick building was that we could use extensive glass surfaces in the facades, giving the building a high degree of generality, and yet the building as a whole would still be energy and climate efficient.

JL: How have you worked with the building's form and expression?

BT & MV: We always start a project by looking for a solution to the program, which from a pragmatic perspective is our actual assignment—a solution that can be formulated without regard to architectural form. Then the building's own logic and potential are developed within the lines of the main concept—spatial relationships, circulation, daylighting, and structure. Opportunities for form and design emerge as a consequence of that working method rather than being a starting point, although in practice the process isn't really linear. In this case, we discovered that the rounded contours of the plan give a visual impression of shortening the length of the facades and connecting the roofline to the surrounding buildings. The rust-red corten steel cladding has intentionally been given a depth that gives the building weight despite its very large glazed areas. Vertical loads are transmitted through what appear as solid fields that shift from top to bottom, countering the traditional static image of how a building's mass is distributed. Our objective has been to create a concentrated building that uses contemporary construction methods to achieve the level of detail and materiality found in the handmade brickwork (of the surrounding KTH campus buildings). On the interior we're looking for clear and specific spaces without sacrificing generality. To achieve this, we work with daylight, scale, and form. For creating generality we work with generous dimensions and contiguous areas that allow the spaces to be used in a variety of ways over the life of the building.

JL: What do you think about architectural education in that regard? And how does it relate to other disciplines—in terms of space and in general?

BT & MV: Architecture school is less about assimilating and then directly applying previously established knowledge than other degree programs are. Instead, its purpose is to develop a student's ability to make good decisions and to navigate correctly without access to or overview of all of the facts. And to create values beyond the strictly necessary. Aalto described this by calling the architect a generalist—there's always someone who knows more about each of the specialist disciplines encompassed by architecture. And yet it's the architect's job to formulate the best overall solution. Spatially, an architecture school—in Sweden, at least—is characterized by the almost constant presence of students in the design studios, which places extreme demands on the design of the building.

JL: What is your opinion of the other architecture schools in Sweden—the ones we've already touched on, and the new one in Umeå?

BT & MV: Zimdal, Henriksson, and Anselm's work had a matter-of-factness and a kind of rational ambition that we admire—a desire to be clear all the way from the overall whole to the smallest detail. And also that their buildings represent the time in which they were built. We've only visited Henning Larsen and White's building in Umeå once, and that was before it was fully occupied. What impressed us the most was the attempt to create great spaciousness and openness between the different floor levels and classrooms—a kind of industrial loft surrounding an oversized stair-case in the middle. But it seemed problematic for the school's activities, especially acoustically, with so little closed-off space in relation to the open areas. But hopefully the basic structure is robust enough to tolerate additional closed-off spaces where the need arises.

JL: Finally, how have you thought about, and what is your view of, the significance of the spatial environment to the study of architecture?

BT & MV: Simply put, it's about not locking in the teaching to a certain educational structure, to fixed class sizes and so forth. When it comes to developing a success-ful educational culture in an architecture school, it depends less on the building than on the administration and its resources. The ideal would be teaching in studios led by practicing and writing architects, and with enough instructors and researchers to also be able to produce publications and exhibitions as part of the curriculum. That way you can achieve enough critical mass for the discussion of architectural strate-gies and intensions to make an impression and have an influence on what we build. That has to be the goal.

The interview is a revised version of the previously published text; Johan Linton, Bolle Tham, Martin Videgård, "Arkitekturskola," Psykoanalytisk Tid/Skrift, *28–29 (2009).*

Johan Linton is an architect, architectural historian and researcher. He is a cofounder of Psykoanalytisk Tid/Skrift, a cultural journal with a significant architectural component (starting in 2011, its new title is Arche). *He is also a designer and artist whose work is represented in various museums in Scandinavia.*

List of Projects

2010

Bergman Center, Fårö, Gotland, Client: Fårö Bergman Center Foundation, 1,300 m², Project: 2010–, Invited competition: 2010, 1st prize

Circuit House, Fiskebäckskil, Lysekil, Client: Private, 70 m², Project: 2010–

Djursholms Ösby, Housing Competition, Stockholm, Client: Private, Project: 2010

Electron Microscope, Linköping University, Client: Akademiska Hus Öst, 400 m², Project: 2010–, Planned realization: 2011

Simrishamn Apartments, Client: Private, 800 m², Project: 2010–

Västra Lagnö, Summerhouse, Stockholm Archipelago, Client: Private, 140 m², Project: 2010–

Vällingby Parkstad, Housing Competition, Client: Sveafastigheter, 15,500 m², Project: 2010

2009

Åhléns Department Store, Uppsala, Client: Axfast, 11,000 m², Project: 2009–, Planned realization: 2012

Childrens atelier, The Swedish Museum of Architecture, Stockholm, Client: The Swedish Museum of Architecture, 100 m², Project: 2009–10, Completion: 2010

Cloud Chamber, Victoria & Albert Museum, London, UK, Client: V&A Contemporary, 16 m², Project: 2009–10

Ekerum Golf and Resort, Urban Planning and Housing, Öland, Client: PEAB, 45,000 m², Project: 2009–

Emergency Architecture, Crossing: Dialogues for Emergency Architecture, Beijing, Client: NAMOC, National Art Museum of China, Exhibition: 2009

House House, Husarö, Stockholm Archipelago, 200 m², Project: 2009, Planned realization: 2011

Linnaeus University, Kalmar, Urban Planning, Client: Kalmar University, 40,000 m², Project: 2009

Naturum Laponia, Visitors centre for Stuor Muorkke, Laponia world heritage area, Sweden, Client: County Administrative Board of Norrbotten, 900 m², Invited competition: 2009

NOTCH 09, Architectural installation, Beijing, Client: NOTCH Festival, 75 m², Project: 2009

Solna Centrum, Urban planning, Client: Solna Municipality and Unibail Rodamco, 80,000 m², Project: 2009–

Double Helix Tower, Observation Deck and Information Center, Barkarby, Järfälla, Client: Järfälla Municipality, Project: 2009–, Invited competition: 2011, 1st prize

Stockholm Concert Hall, Client: Stockholm Concert Hall Foundation and Locum, 4,000 m², Project: 2009–, Invited competition: 2010, 1st prize

Vertical Village, Urban planning and Housing, Hässelby, Stockholm, Client: Veidekke, 4,500 m², Project: 2009

Västra Kajen, Housing, Munksjön, Jönköping, Client: Vätterhem and Riksbyggen, 9,000 m², Project: 2009–, Invited competition: 2009, 1st prize

Warfvinges väg, Office and Housing, Kungsholmen, Stockholm, Client: Sätila holding, 2,000 m², Project: 2009–

2008

15 m², Kit houses, Client: Sommarnöjen, 15 m², Project: 2008–

Brick House, Skåne, Client: Private, 270 m², Project: 2008–

Hotel Anno 1647, Södermalm, Stockholm, Client: Hotel Anno 1647, In collaboration with Thiel arkitekter, 2,500 m², Project: 2008

Gribbe-Erich House, Älgö, Stockholm, Client: Private, 330 m², Project: 2008–, Planned realization: 2010

Ljunggren-Sundberg House, Visby, Gotland, Client: Private, 300 m², Project: 2007–

Åkesson House, Stavsnäs, Stockholm, Client: Private, 160 m², Project: 2008–

Moderna Museet Malmö, Client: Stadsfastigheter Malmö and Moderna museet, 3,500 m², Project: 2008, Completion: 2009

Ordos 100, Parcel 12, Inner Mongolia, China, Curator: Ai Weiwei with Herzog & de Meuron, Client: Jiang Yuan Water Engineering Ltd., 1,000 m², Project: 2008–, Planned realization: 2011

Power plant, Örebro, Client: E. ON Sverige AB, 9,000 m², Project: 2008

Community space Conversion, Bagarmossen, Client: Riksrådsvägen Housing Co-operative, 90 m², Project: 2008, Completion: 2009

Top, Lamp series, Manufacturer: Zero, Design: 2008

Tree Hotel, Harads, Boden, Client: Brittas pensionat, 16 m², Project: 2008–10

Tumba Housing and Urban Planning, Botkyrka, Client: Tumba Municipality, Project: 2008

Humblegatan, Lilla Alby, Housing, Sundbyberg, Client: Wåhlin Fastigheter, 8,000 m², Project: 2008, Planned realization: 2013

2007

AH043 Housing, Lidingö, Client: Arkitekthus, 8 x 250 m², Project: 2007, Completion: 2008

Beckasinen, Housing, Östermalm, Stockholm, Client: Sveamalm Fastigheter, 1,400 m², Project: 2007–08, Completion: 2009

Bryggvägen, Urban Planning and Housing, Gröndal, Stockholm, Client: Byggvesta, 30,000 m², Project: 2007

Södertälje Urban Planning, Client: Telge Fastigheter, 14,500 m², Project: 2007

Exhibition for the Asplund Library Competition, The Swedish Museum of Architecture, Stockholm, 560 m², Project: 2007, Completion: 2007

House B-1, Skälderviken, Skåne, Client: Private, 360 m², Project: 2007

Ekudden House, Vindö, Stockholm Archipelago, Client: Private, 330 m², Project: 2007

Ljungren House, Visby, Gotland, Client: Private, 300 m², Project: 2007–

House L-S, Visby, Gotland, Client: Private, 300 m², Project: 2007–

Ugglero House, Extension, Kungsängen, Client: Liljedahl-af Ugglas family, 80 m², Project: 2007, Completion: 2008

Tellus Nursery School, Telefonplan, Client: Wasakronan, 1,250 m², Project: 2007–09, Completion: 2010

Pool House, Project for the Book 15 Kvadrat, 15 m², Project: 2007

School of Architecture, and Campus Entrance Building, The Royal Institute of Technology, Stockholm, Client: Akademiska Hus Stockholm, 13,200 m², Project: 2007–, Invited competition: 2007, 1st prize, Planned realization: 2013

2006

Botanic Garden House, Skälderviken, Skåne, Client: Private, 300 m², Project: 2006

Cliff House, Skåne, Client: Private, 250 m², Project: 2006

DDB Office, Vasastan, Stockholm, Client: DDB Stockholm, 1,500 m², Project: 2006–07, Completion: 2007

Eriksvik Housing, Housing, Nacka, Stockholm, 480 m², Client: Arkitekthus, Project: 2006–07, Completion: 2008

Garden House, Viksberg, Södertälje, Client: Elisabeth Krausz, Peter A Sjögren, 240 m² + glass house, Project: 2006–07, Completion: 2008

Glasberga Housing, Urban Planning and Housing, Södertälje, Client: FKTS, 10,000 m², Project: 2006–07

House C, Särö, Client: Kim and Kajsa Cramer, 240 m², Project: 2006–07, Completion: 2007

Humlegården Apartment, Östermalm, Stockholm, Client: Private, 375 m², Project: 2006–08, Completion: 2008

Lejdström House, Edsviken, Sollentuna, Client: Private, 270 m², Project: 2006

Stensmyr House, Arild, Skåne, Client: Private, 130 m², Project: 2006

Vigeland House, Oslo, Norway, Addition and Conversion, Client: Saethre-Furuholmen family, 126 + 276 m², Project: 2006

Husarö Summerhouse, Stockholm Archipelago, Client: Private, 110 m², Project: 2006–

Styrsö Housing, Styrsö Island, Göteborg, Client: Styrsö Utveckling AB, 5,500 m², Project: 2006–, Planned completion: 2013

The Middle Kingdom, Permanent exhibition, Stockholm, Client: Museum of far Eastern Antiquities, 560 m², Project: 2005-2007, Invited competition: 2005, 1st prize, Completion: 2007

2005

AH042, Kit house, Client: Arkitekthus, 200 m², Project: 2005

Double Houses, Gavelvägen, Lidingö, 580 m², Project: 2005–06, Completion: 2006

Gateau, Bread and bakery stand, Sturegallerian, Stockholm, 16 m², Client: Gateau, Project: 2005, Completion: 2005

House BLG, Killinge, Lidingö, Client: Breeze-Le Guellaff family, 150 m², Project: 2005–06, Completion: 2006

Ingerstedt Apartment, Kungsholmen, Stockholm, Client: Private, 100 m², Project: 2005, Completion: 2005

S Apartment, Östermalm, Stockholm, Client: Private, 180 m², Project: 2005, Completion: 2006

Söderöra, Summerhouse, Stockholm Archipelago, Client: Private, 81 m², Project: 2005–06, Completion: 2008

2004

Böler Kirke, Church and Parish Center, Oslo, Norway, 2,000 m², Open international competition: 2004

Double House, Nora, Danderyd, Client: H Larsson, 400 m², Project: 2004, Completion: 2005

House K, Stocksund, Danderyd, Client: Private, 240 m², Project: 2004, Completion: 2005

Kalmar Museum of Art, Stadsparken, Kalmar, Client: Kalmar Municipality, 1,600 m², Open international competition: 2004, 1st prize, Project: 2004–06, Completion: 2008

2003

Archipelago House, Husarö, Stockholm archipelago, Client: Tomas Tjajkovski, 130 m² + 20 m² boat house, Project: 2003–05, Completion: 2006

Church in Fruängen, Stockholm, 205 m², Open international competition: 2003, Honourable Mention

Djurgårdsbrunn, Restaurant and Housing, Djurgården, Stockholm, Client: H Larsson, 800 m², Project 2003

Houses J & S, Hässelby, Stockholm, 360 m², Project: 2003, Completion: 2004

2002

Almada, Urban Planning, Lisnave shipyard site, Lisbon, Portugal, Team with Prof Arch Klas Tham, Client: Municipio de Almada, 50 ha, 750,000 m², Invited international competition: 2002

Apartment Hamberger, Östermalm, Stockholm, Client: Private, 108 m², Project: 2002, Completion: 2003

Atrium House, Summerhouse, Gotland, Client: Private, 250 m², Project: 2002–10, Completion: 2010

House BS-1, Ekerö, Client: Private, 260 m², Project: 2002

House BS-2, Ekerö, Client: Private, 270 m², Project: 2002–03, Completion: 2005

Stable House, Conversion, Östermalm, Stockholm, In collaboration with Olof Söderholm, Client: Larsson family, Project: 2002, Completion: 2003

Stationshuset, Restaurant and Organic Store, Saltsjöbaden, Client: Voltaire/Blom/Enander, 180 m², Project: 2002, Completion: 2003

Tiles Apartment, Vasastan, Stockholm, Client: Private, 95 m², Project: 2002–03, Completion: 2003

T&V / Sweden, Office, Södermalm, Stockholm, Client: TVH and Sweden Graphics, 200 m², Project: 2002, Completion: 2002

2001

Blom House, Kummelnäs, Nacka, Client: Viveka Blom-Nygren, 360 m², Project: 2001–02, Completion: 2003

House Z, Edsviken, Danderyd, Client: Private, 400 m², Project: 2001–02

Royal Theatre, Copenhagen, Denmark, 75,000 m², Open international competition: 2001

Kvarteret Skutan, Housing and Offices, Extention and Conversion, Industrigatan, Stockholm, Client: Fastighetsaktiebolaget Stockholmia, 2,600 m², Project: 2001–02

Snowcrasch, Office and Showroom, Hammarby, Stockholm, External collaborator: Ulrika Ljungberg, Client: Art & Technology by Proventus, 1,250 m², Project: 2001, Completion: 2001

2000

Bergström Apartment, Södermalm, Stockholm, Client: Private, 155 m², Project: 2000–2001, Completion: 2002

Biolab, Microbiological laboratory, New England, USA, 20,000 m², Open international competition: 2000

Karlsson House, Tidö-Lindö, Västerås, Client: Björn and Berit Karlsson, 180 m², Project: 2000–02, Completion: 2002

Leca House, 145 m², Idea competition: 2000

Orgelfabriken, Apartment conversion, Norrmalm, Stockholm, Client: Saethre-Furuholmen family, 175 m², Project: 2000, Completion: 2001

Schumacher Summerhouse, Älgö, Stockholm Archipelago, Client: Private, 15 m², Project: 2000–01

1999

Restaurant Box, Stureplan, Stockholm, Client: Gateau, 18 m², Project: 1999–2000, Completion: 2000

Ugglero House, Kungsängen, Stockholm, Client: Liljedahl-af Ugglas family, 170 m², Project: 1999–2001, Completion: 2002

Apartment Hellström Nevander, Östermalm, Stockholm, Client: Private, 73 m², Project: 1999, Completion: 2000

City Library, Turkku, Finland, 10,400 m², Open international competition: 1999, shortlisted

Awards and Nominations

2011

Double Helix Tower, Observation Deck and Information Center, Barkarby, Invited competition, 1st prize.

2010

Bergman Center, Invited competition, 1st prize.
Stockholm Concert Hall. Invited competition, 1st prize.
Moderna Museet Malmö shortlisted for World's Best New Cultural Building at the World Architecture Festival (ES).

2009

Västra Kajen, invited competition, 1st prize.
Kalmar Museum of Art shortlisted for the Mies van der Rohe Award 2009, the European Union Prize for Contemporary Architecture.
Tham & Videgård Arkitekter selected for Architectural Record's "Design Vanguard 2009," the annual list of the world's top 10 emerging architects.

2008

Kalmar Museum of Art shortlisted for World's Best New Cultural Building at the World Architecture Festival (ES).
Garden House awarded Best New Building—the Building of the Year—in the Södertälje region.
Double House nominated by the international jury for the Ecola Awards in Germany.

2007

The New School of Architecture, Royal institute of Technology-KTH, Stockholm, Sweden. Invited competition, 1st prize.
Archipelago House nominated for Best Wooden Building in Sweden 2004–08.

2005

Kalmar Museum of Art, Open international competition, 1st prize.
New Permanent Exhibition on Chinese Art & Culture, Museum of Far Eastern Antiquities. Invited competition, 1st prize.
Tham & Videgård Arkitekter awarded Residence Magazine Architects of the Year.

2004

Karlsson House nominated for Best Wooden Building in Sweden.

2003

Church in Fruängen, open international competition, Honorable mention.

2001

Snowcrash Office and Showroom, Stockholm, 1st prize CoreDesign.

1999

New City Library of Turkku, Finland, open international competition, shortlisted.

Exhibitions

2011

Louisiana Museum of Modern Art;
Living, Arkitekturens grænser III-IV: Tree Hotel, Garden House and Ordos 100.

2010

Lisbon Architecture Triennale, exhibition dedicated to the house, the dwelling, curated by Peter Cook, Portugal.
12th International Venice Biennale "People meet in Architecture" curated by Kazuyo Sejima, Nordic Pavillion, Venice, Italy.
00–tal, The Swedish Museum of Architecture, Stockholm.
1:1–Architects Build Small Spaces, Victoria & Albert Museum, Architecture 2010 exhibition, London UK.
BINA 2010, Housing Models: Experimentation and Everyday Life, Artget gallery, Cultural center of Belgrade, Serbia.

2009

NOTCH 09, architectural piece at the culture festival in Beijing, China.
The Mies van der Rohe Award 2009, touring European exhibition.
ART Basel—Ordos 100 house project, Basel, Switzerland.
Crossing: Dialogues for Emergency Architecture, National Art Museum of China, Beijing.

2008

Best Wooden Building in Sweden, touring exhibition 2008–10.
Greener than thou, exhibition on Swedish contemporary architecture in London, UK.
Les Maison Rouge, Swedish Institute of Culture in Paris, France.

2007

44 Young Architects Exhibition and Publication, Barcelona and Santiago de Compostela, Spain.
Archipelago House included in the permanent collection at the Swedish Museum of Architecture.
Housing in the Nordic Countries at Frederiks Bastion, Copenhagen, Denmark.

2006

House AH041 presented by Swedish type house company Arkitekthus at the Salone de Mobile, Milan, Italy.

2005

Young Swedish Architecture, A new generation of architects at the Swedish Museum of Architecture, Stockholm.

2004

Best Wooden Building in Sweden, touring exhibition, opened at Formens Hus, Malmö.

Martin Videgård

Born 1968 in Stockholm

Education

University of Stockholm, Art history 1990–91.
University College of Arts, Crafts, and Design,
Stockholm 1992–94.
Universidade do Porto Faculty of Architecture,
Portugal 1996.
Royal Institute of Technology, Architecture,
Stockholm 1994–97.

Work

Can Arkitektkontor 1987–88
Berg Arkitektkontor 1989–90
Nyrens Arkitekter 1995
Wilhelmson Arkitekter 1997–99
Own practice 1996–99
Tham & Videgård Arkitekter 1999–

Other

Swedish Association of Architects,
member of the board 2010–

Bolle Tham

Born 1970 in Stockholm

Education

Royal Institute of Technology, Architecture,
Stockholm 1991–97.
Ecole d'Architecture de Paris Belleville,
Paris, France 1994–95.
ILAUD, International Laboratory for Architecture
and Urban Design
San Marino / Urbino, Italy 1996.
The Royal University College of Fine Arts,
Faculty of Architecture, Post Graduate studies,
Stockholm 1998–99

Work

Reichen & Robert Architectes, Paris 1994–95
Own practice 1996–99
Tham & Videgård Arkitekter 1999–

Other

Architects Association of Stockholm,
member of the board 2004–08

Collaborators

March 2011

Andreas Helgesson, Anna Jacobson,
Anna-Lisa Pollock, Carmen Izquierdo Làzaro,
Johanna Redell, Konrad Krupinski, Lukas Thiel,
Mia Nygren, Mårten Nettelbladt, Pau Boluda
Hernandez.

1991–

Benjamin Mandre, Eric Engström, Marina Rotolo,
Chris Paxton, Andy Penuela, Marina Huguet
Blasi, Christine Lavelid, Julia Gudiel Urbano,
Jamie Hay, Laura O Brien, Harriet Brisley,
Suzanne Prest, Karolina Nyström, Marcus
Andrén, Susanna Bremberg, Helene Amundsen,
Fredrik Nilsson, Tove Belfrage, Anna-Katharina
Koss, Colin Harper, Erik Wåhlström, Josefine
Wikholm, Caroline Carlsson, Lisette Bramsell,
Mattias Antonsson, Johan Björkholm, Anders
Rognerud, Elin Andreassen, Helena Hemminger,
Carl Lindman, Henrik Lundén, Måns Tham,
John Billberg, Claes Sörstedt, Fredrik Olson,
Therese Drougge, Maria Lundqvist.

Modelmakers

Mårten Ubbe, Ola Ek (Kalmar Museum of Art,
Brick House, Cloud Chamber, Bergmancenter)
Andreas Hedenskog (Ugglero House, Blom
House, Karlsson House, Archipelago house)

Editor
Johan Linton

Production
Henrik Nygren Design

Project coordination
Robert Steiger, Odine Oßwald (Birkhäuser Verlag)

Translation from Swedish into English
John Krause

Photography
Åke E:son Lindman (works), Åsa Lundén,
Mikael Olsson, Tham & Videgård Arkitekter,
Lars Wallsten

A CIP catalogue record for this book is available
from the Library of Congress, Washington D.C.,
USA.

Bibliographic information published by the
German National Library

The German National Library lists this publication
in the Deutsche Nationalbibliografie; detailed
bibliographic data are available on the Internet at
http://dnb.d-nb.de.

© 2011 Birkhäuser GmbH, Basel
P.O. Box, CH-4002 Basel, Switzerland
Part of ActarBirkhäuser

Sales: ActarBirkhäuserD
Barcelona - Basel - New York
www.actarbirkhauser-d.com

Printed on acid-free paper produced from
chlorine-free pulp. TCF ∞

Printed by Fälth & Hässler, Värnamo, Sweden.

ISBN 978–3–0346–0688–2

9 8 7 6 5 4 3 2 1

www.birkhauser.com